Antagonists may be a part of any congregation. To deal with antagonistic situations in a proactive manner is honest, positive leadership that is vital to congregational life and growth!

THE REV. TIM BAUER
Clarks Grove, Minnesota

This book is an eye opener. It points out the significance of having organization, policies, and an apparatus in place to deal with problems before they become major antagonistic matters.

ROBERT BERTHELSEN
Albert Lea, Minnesota

This book helped me greatly. I believe it can help save pastors and churches.

THE REV. DAVID MUSTIAN
Boulder, Colorado

Many of the chapters seemed written for me personally. The book has given me courage and validation ... not to mention a big PUSH!

LINDA E. RETZLAFF
Fayetteville, Georgia

ANTAGONISTS
in the Church

Kenneth C. Haugk

ANTAGONISTS
in the Church

How to Identify and Deal with Destructive Conflict

AUGSBURG Publishing House • Minneapolis

ANTAGONISTS IN THE CHURCH
How to Identify and Deal with Destructive Conflict

Copyright © 1988 Kenneth C. Haugk

This book is accompanied by a 64-page study guide suitable for use by either individuals or groups: *Antagonists in the Church Study Guide* by Kenneth C. Haugk and R. Scott Perry (Minneapolis: Augsburg, 1988).

Scripture quotations unless otherwise noted are from the Revised Standard Version of the Bible, copyright 1946, 1952, and 1971 by the Division of Christian Education of the National Council of Churches.

Scripture quotations marked Phillips are from The New Testament in Modern English, copyright 1958, 1959, 1960, 1972 by J. B. Phillips.

Library of Congress Cataloging-in-Publication Data

Haugk, Kenneth C., 1945-
   ANTAGONISTS IN THE CHURCH

   1. Church controversies. I. Title.
BV652.9.H37 1988   253   88-6354
ISBN 0-8066-2310-1

Manufactured in the U.S.A.   APH 10-0372

99   98   97   96   95   11   12   13   14   15   16   17   18   19

To caring Christians everywhere who
suffer the attacks of antagonists,
long for peace,
strive for justice,
love their neighbors,
and desire to follow our Lord
wherever he leads.

Contents

Preface

*T*HE HEART and soul of this book are *care* and *hope.*

This is a book of care: care for congregations, care for leaders, care for members, and care for those who are antagonists. Sooner or later most congregations experience some degree of destructive conflict caused by antagonism. Such conflict, though caused by so few, has the potential to disrupt, even to destroy, the mission and ministry of Jesus Christ through the people of God. But even in the midst of that conflict, congregations and their leaders have a unique opportunity to care deeply.

This is also a book of hope: hope for congregations, hope for leaders of congregations, hope for members, and hope for pastors. When readers understand and apply the principles of this book, they can prevent or at least reduce much of the pain and suffering caused by antagonism. Even in the midst of unhealthy antagonistic conflict, congregations and their leaders can grow in hope.

For a decade prior to writing this book, I conducted workshops on church antagonism and what to do about it for pastors, lay leaders, denominational officials, seminarians, and the spouses of all of them. During these workshops I heard many reports of the bitter harm antagonists can cause in congregations. My experience as a clinical psychologist, working with individuals who have been severely hurt by antagonistic situations, bore this out as well. I also saw the good that can result when people receive appropriate information on the subject.

The intent of this book is to make appropriate information about antagonism more widely available. But such information is sensitive because it deals with sensitive topics.

Antagonistic individuals require a firm response. Among the subjects discussed in these pages is the necessity of confrontation, which is uncomfortable for many Christians. I believe that the goal must be to show great care and concern for all involved—including antagonists—without sacrificing firmness.

While this book includes some "tough love" prescriptions, my hope is that congregations will always be places where the love of Christ is evident. Care and hope have been mine in the writing, and care and hope are equally necessary as you read this book and apply its principles.

My hope is that this book will enable you to know precisely which firm and loving steps to take in dealing with antagonists, and that these methods will reduce instances of antagonism for the good of all and thereby contribute to building up the body of Christ.

My hope is that you will adapt the contents of this book to fit your own style and strengths. The method used here is to *overtrain* you to deal with antagonists. Once you know how to deal with the most troublesome minority—antagonists of the first magnitude—you will also be equipped to deal with those who are less severely antagonistic.

My hope is that Christian congregations will be places of God's peace and power, ministering effectively to the world without the disruptive influence of antagonists to distract them from their calling. The chapters on prevention are particularly important for congregational ministry because they can help you establish an environment where antagonism is much less likely to occur.

My hope is also for antagonists themselves, that as a result of firm, loving confrontation some will be helped toward healthy change. Although change in a full-fledged antagonist is rare, all things are possible for God, and the techniques contained in this book can be used to offer antagonists some hope of recognizing their behavior for what it is—and possibly changing.

In the face of Christ's commands to love our enemies and turn the other cheek, congregations have sometimes been confused and even baffled as they have tried to deal effectively with antagonists. This book is a practical, loving effort to sort out that confusion. I commend you for taking the task seriously, and I pray that this volume will be a valuable tool for your life and ministry.

Unless otherwise noted, the stories told in this book are composites of a variety of different situations, and the names used are fictitious. However, these stories reflect the actual dynamics of experiences with church antagonists.

Acknowledgments

*T*HE CONCEPTS and applications in this book have been developed over a period of 10 years, during which time they have been augmented by insights gained in workshops, lectures, consultations, and personal experience with antagonists. During this long gestation period the book manuscript was reviewed at various stages by many persons. The life and work experiences of numerous individuals are also reflected in these pages though, for reasons of confidentiality, they cannot be named. I am sure that even if I attempted to name them, I would overlook some who offered validation or helpful suggestions. They all know who they are, however, and I am immensely grateful to them all, clergy and lay persons alike.

I also appreciate the feedback I received from the leaders and participants who pilot-tested this book and its companion study guide in their congregations. Many refinements and clarifications came out of that extensive field-testing effort, and I am grateful to each and every one who took part.

More than 40 church officials, representing 19 denominations, reviewed Chapter 21, "Denominational Support Structures." Many of these denominational leaders also read the manuscript in its entirety and made helpful comments. The book is the better for the ministrations of these willing servants.

There are two individuals whom I particularly wish to thank, since they provided significant help in formulating a beginning theoretical basis for this book and motivation to work in the area. Wayne Oates first prompted me to delve into this subject when I read the chapter, "Ministering to Extremists" in his book *Pastoral Counseling in Social Problems.* In addition, I am grateful to Speed Leas of the Alban Institute for his description of "Levels of Conflict in the Church" in his work *Moving Your Church through Conflict.*

Finally, I appreciate the work of my colleague and my friend Scott Perry, who coauthored the study guide and provided valuable feedback on the book manuscript as well.

Part One
DEFINING THE ISSUE

Hope Is the Beginning

*A*NTAGONISM is a reality. It leaves in its wake broken lives and people who are hurt, discouraged, and apathetic toward the new life in Christ. Antagonism is as real a phenomenon as the feelings described in this journal of a lay leader:

At first I thought it was funny. Surely no one could take him seriously. He sounded like a broken record, going over and over the same material. *Do nothing,* I thought, *and he'll go away.*

Later I began to realize it was no laughing matter. I was shocked to hear the rumors he was spreading about me. Some time after I discovered the source of those rumors, I remember meeting him on the way downstairs to the fellowship hall. The light was burned out, so I didn't see who was coming up the narrow stairway until he stopped to let me pass. He wore a tight smirk on his face. I was so overpowered by hurt and anger when I saw him, I felt stirrings of nausea. The year's worth of pain I had absorbed welled up inside me. I hated him!

Knowing I could hate that much staggered me—and in

church, right after worship. I felt so guilty. Once again, briefly, I found myself thinking that surely this man would respond to friendly overtures. Maybe if I explained my position one more time, he would understand. Maybe I just wasn't a good enough Christian, or open enough to explain my thoughts and feelings clearly. I just couldn't reach him.

At that moment the solution became painfully clear to me. The church had suffered enough hurt and upset already. The only thing I could do was resign as council chairman. Then maybe the church could get on with its ministry. I don't know if I can even stay on as a member of my church. Every time I would see that smug, self-satisfied look on his face, my stomach would turn.

I can't see any other way out of the bind. I never thought I was the type to get an ulcer, but the last few weeks I've had heartburn every night.

Antagonism can obliterate a sense of the presence of God's love in individuals and in the faith community. It is an affliction of the whole people of God. Perhaps antagonism most frequently tears into the lives of church staff members. Here is what one pastor had to say about the trauma of antagonism:

I just feel angry sometimes. Angry at that individual, angry at the congregation and the leaders for seemingly deserting me, angry at myself, and sometimes livid with God for allowing this to happen.

Mostly though, I feel afraid. Very much afraid. I'm afraid of being unable to cope. Afraid of what people will say. Afraid I'll lose my job—and yet sometimes I feel like quitting, just throwing in the towel and saying, "There, God. If you won't take care of me, then forget about me taking care of them."

And I feel sorry for myself, then ashamed when I realize I'm dreaming about revenge. That's not me. But it *is* me. The whole thing upsets me so much that I'm obsessed with it. I get so I can't sleep at night. The longer it has worn on, the more tense I have grown. Sometimes I feel like I'm going to explode. It has spread slowly, like poison, to contaminate every part of my life. I'm irritable at home and church, suspicious of almost everyone. It seems as if I'm turning into the kind of person the antagonist says I am.

And then the awful doubts come. Maybe the antagonist is right. Maybe I should leave and let someone else take over. So I slip into depression until I get so angry that I fight my way out of it. And the process repeats itself like a hideous roller coaster ride that never ends.

I don't know what to do.

Antagonism in action is not pleasant. It is a harsh reality, yet one that must be reckoned with. *There are those who wantonly, selfishly, and destructively attack others.* In a congregation, that can mean repeated disruption of boards, committees, and the entire congregation. Antagonism leaves in its wake not only incidental damage, but often deep and extensive destruction. It is this severity of damage that makes it essential that the church learn about antagonism.

Antagonism should not be confused with mere criticism or healthy conflict in the church. People sometimes use the word *antagonists* simply as a description of people on different sides in an argument. That is not the use here intended for the word. Such "antagonists" would not likely be responsible for the kind of hurt and brokenness evident in the above vignettes. For healthy conflict the church would do well to adopt the terminology of the British Parliament, calling those in differing camps the "Honorable Opposition."

Antagonism is *unhealthy* conflict, however, and antagonistic behavior is *not* honorable. The word will be defined and used throughout this book in this way:

Antagonists are individuals who, on the basis of nonsubstantive evidence, go out of their way to make insatiable

---

demands, usually attacking the person or performance of others. These attacks are selfish in nature, tearing down rather than building up, and are frequently directed against those in a leadership capacity.

Words can hardly express the tragedy of antagonism. Where a broken world ought to be able to say about Christians, "See how they love one another" (Tertullian), sometimes the scenes played out in public lead people to say rather, "They fight more than the rest of us put together!"

Yet even in the midst of antagonism there is some hope. There is hope because you can learn to *recognize* antagonism, *prevent* antagonism, and *deal with* antagonism.

Part One of this book will help you define antagonism, differentiate it from ordinary conflict (which is often healthy), understand why churches make particularly good breeding grounds for antagonists, and see the problem in the context of the Bible and the ethical issues involved.

The chapters included in Part Two constitute a manual for identifying the characteristics, behaviors, and warning signals of an antagonist. They explain how to recognize whether or not a person is an antagonist by observing that person's behavior and history.

Part Three deals with the all-important subject of prevention—how to create an environment and a support structure that will minimize the likelihood of antagonism rearing its head in your congregation.

In Part Four you will learn strategies, skills, and techniques that will help you cope with antagonism should it arise.

As you read, you will note an underlying assumption, namely that the primary audience for this book includes pastors and lay leaders who are confronted by antagonism within a congregation. Of course, the fact is that antagonism can come *from leaders* as well. Much of this book—95 percent or more—will apply in either event. From time to time, however, I will note differences in approach that would be necessary when a leader is an antagonist.

Another point to consider is, *Whose problem is it when an antagonist is raising Cain in the church?* The question is not who is causing the problem. The antagonist is. The question is rather, *Who is responsible for dealing with the antagonist and the problems he or she causes?* The answer is, *everyone.* Whether one is a pastor, another staff person, a lay leader, or simply a member of the congregation, all are responsible collectively.

Oftentimes committed Christians (clergy and lay persons) possess the personality trait of altruism or selfless giving. Occasionally, this trait, which can be quite positive, can lead church leaders into overcommitment or even messianic attitudes: "*I* am the fix-it person, *I* am the healer, *I* must do all the dirty, difficult, or unpleasant tasks." Deeply committed people often feel obligated to deal single-handedly with an antagonist: "It is my problem, I have to be able to take it, I have to deal with it alone."

When one individual assumes the whole burden of dealing with an antagonist, the result is rarely healthy. The obligation to deal with the situation properly resides in the corporate leadership of the congregation and, to a lesser extent, in the congregation as a whole.

A congregation is uniquely structured to undertake this obligation, because a church is a body—Christ's body—and is considerably more than the sum of its parts. It resembles an organism more than an organization, pulsing with the very life of Jesus flowing through its members by means of the Holy Spirit. Antagonism is like a virulent disease in that body. A body cannot regard attack on a single part as an inconsequential threat requiring no response by other parts. Antagonism poses a threat not only to an isolated organ, but also to the entire organism, which suffers until the disease is overcome. The whole body must work to overcome it.

Apathy can also be an obstacle. Apathy causes people to close their eyes and say, "Don't get involved." "Keep the peace at any price." Apathy lulls people into saying, "Wait—wait until trouble or danger affects me personally." Apathy in the church can lead to members saying, "Sure, so-and-so is an antagonist, but it's not bothering *me*. Live and let live, I say. Let somebody else handle it." Remember, however, that conflict with an antagonist is an attack by hostile forces on the very life of the church. All must work together to repel the attack, though by the very nature of their function, leaders will generally assume a more active role than others.

Whose problem is antagonism? It's *everyone's* problem. In the ark of salvation that is the church, no one can afford to say, "Your end of the boat is sinking." An attitude that "We are all in this together" provides an immensely powerful, effective antidote to the disruptive poisons of antagonism. It is also a chief source of hope. The learning of skills for dealing with antagonists and methods for preventing their attacks is another source of hope. And finally, the church is the Lord's. He has called it into being and he will not fail it. Here is hope beyond measure.

What Is Church Antagonism?

*B*EING a Christian: is it difficult or easy? The answer is that it is both. Jesus said on the one hand, "In the world you have tribulation" (John 16:33). But he also declared, "... my yoke is easy, and my burden is light" (Matt. 11:30).

Being a Christian is difficult. Being a Christian is easy. Both statements are true, although neither tells the whole truth by itself.

Nowhere are the difficulties of being a Christian more evident than in dealing with the problem of church antagonism. Nowhere are "easy yokes" and "light burdens" less evident than in a congregation choked and crushed by the presence of antagonism.

What is church antagonism? It is that disruption in a congregation caused by an antagonist, as defined in Chapter 1:

Antagonists are individuals who, on the basis of *nonsubstantive evidence, go out of their way* to make *insatiable demands,* usually attacking the person or performance of others. These attacks are *selfish in nature, tearing down rather than building up,* and are frequently directed against those in a leadership capacity.

Some key phrases in this definition deserve closer attention:

- *nonsubstantive evidence:* The arguments an antagonist presents are typically founded on little or grossly misrepresented evidence. As Shakespeare wrote in *Henry V,* "The empty vessel makes the greatest sound." Three common logical fallacies antagonists employ are: *pettifogging* (quibbling over straws, providing strong proof of irrelevant points); *extension* (exaggerating the opponent's position); and *argumentum ad ignoratium* (making an assertion that cannot be disproved and then claiming that the inability to disprove it makes it true).

- *go out of their way:* Antagonists initiate trouble; they do not wait for trouble to come along. This often goes hand-in-hand with hypersensitivity on their part. They often take every word and action as a personal attack and respond aggressively. Something as seemingly minor as failing to say good morning to them can be enough to cause their antagonism to flare up. Their response to such an omission would most likely be to wonder what you had against them.

- *insatiable demands:* Antagonists are never satisfied. The proverb, "Give him an inch and he'll take a mile" applies doubly to antagonists. No amount of accommodation on your part (or on the part of a group or a congregation as a whole) will ever suffice. Instead of calming antagonists down, attempts at appeasement encourage them to make more demands. Many antagonists fight on until there is nothing left but rubble. Sometimes even that does not stop them.

- *attacking:* This harsh word is accurately applied to antagonists. Although they may present some valid points, antagonists generally do not offer constructive criticism.

Their implicit goal is control, no matter what the cost may be to others.

• *selfish in nature:* The attacks of antagonists are self-serving. Often they will seize on a slogan or pick some side of a valid issue and pretend that is what they are fighting for. It rarely is. An antagonist will quickly drop a particular slogan or issue once it no longer serves his or her ambitions.

• *tearing down rather than building up:* This is the inevitable result of antagonists' actions. Instead of pulling God's people together, they divide them. Show me a divided and strife-torn congregation, and I will show you a congregation that has one or more antagonists in its midst.

Antagonists are not a homogenous group. It is helpful to distinguish three different types:

(1) hard-core antagonists
(2) major antagonists
(3) moderate antagonists

(Note that the dividing lines between these types are somewhat arbitrary and seldom as distinct as the process of categorization would make them appear.)

Hard-Core Antagonists

Hard-core antagonists are seriously disturbed individuals. They are psychotic—out of touch with reality. Their psychosis is almost always of the paranoid variety, which by its nature is not as easy to detect as other psychoses. Many paranoid individuals can appear normal some (or even most) of the time.

Hard-core antagonists tend to have incredible tenacity and an unbelievable desire to make trouble, as demonstrated by the following true story (details have been changed to ensure anonymity).

For a number of years Reverend Smith served a congregation in Oklahoma. During that time, an antagonist launched a vicious attack against him. Fortunately the situation was handled well, and the antagonist left the congregation after inflicting only minimal damage.

After serving the congregation in Oklahoma for 15 years, Reverend Smith received an opportunity to move to a church in California. He decided to make the move, and felt good about it.

His installation day in the new congregation was festive. A spirit of celebration marked the special afternoon service, attended by well over 1000 people. Following the service and after some picture taking, the new minister and the presiding clergy moved from the church toward a fellowship hall downstairs. As the pastor walked down the stairs, he paused for a moment and looked out over the large group of people milling around waiting for the fellowship meal to begin. Two people caught his eye. The Oklahoma antagonist and his wife had traveled more than 1,500 miles to attend the installation in order to sow discrediting rumors about the new minister.

Such is the persistence of some antagonists. This true story demonstrates the extremes to which a hard-core antagonist is willing to go. It also shows why it is so essential to deal effectively with antagonists.

Hard-core antagonists may be the type of people the apostle Paul had in mind when he warned the leaders of the congregation at Ephesus: "Take heed to yourselves and to all the flock, in which the Holy Spirit has made you overseers. . . . I know that after my departure fierce wolves will come in among you, not sparing the flock" (Acts 20:28-29).

Major Antagonists

The majority of those who fall into the category of *major antagonists* are not as severely disturbed as hard-core antagonists, yet they may at times exhibit similar behaviors. Whereas hard-core antagonists *cannot* be reasoned with because they lack the emotional stability to understand, major antagonists *refuse* to be reasoned with. Major antagonists possess the capability of reasoning with their opponents but decline to exercise it. And the demands of major antagonists, also, are insatiable.

Diagnostically, major antagonists have a character or personality disorder. They carry a great deal of hostility, coupled with an overwhelming drive for power. Although they are not psychotic, their personality problems are most certainly deep-seated, yet they are not out of touch with reality. Major antagonists are not neurotic; neurotics experience anxiety, possibly guilt, and a great deal of dissatisfaction with their problems, and they have a desire to change. Major antagonists do not.

Moderate Antagonists

Two features distinguish *moderate antagonists* from those of the first two types. First, a moderate antagonist lacks the self-starting quality of the others. If you were walking on one side of a street and an antagonist of either of the first two types were on the other, he or she would gladly walk across the street to give you trouble. Moderate antagonists would not go so far out of their way. If you both were walking on the same side of the street, however, the moderate antagonist would certainly take advantage of the opportunity to make trouble for you. In other words, an opportunity must be presented more clearly or closely to a moderate antagonist before he or she becomes actively antagonistic.

Second, moderate antagonists lack the perseverance of the others. No moderate antagonist would show up years later in California—unlike major and hard-core antagonists. Moderate antagonists have personality problems, but their problems are not as severe as those of hard-core antagonists or major antagonists. They do make

good *followers* of hard-core and major antagonists, however.

Antagonists of all three types are malevolent in both
intent and effect. You will have no trouble distinguishing
antagonists from *activists,* who are devoted to causes of
some sort and push for change in society's thinking or
behavior. Even if you happen to disagree with the sub-
stance of a cause promoted by activists, it will be evident
that they are committed to the issue. They really care.
They want action, no doubt, but they are *issue*-oriented,
not *person*-oriented. They do not at all fit into the preceding definition of an antagonist, nor do they fit any of
the three types.

It should also be noted that *everyone acts antagonistically at times.* There are times when everyone acts
selfishly, destructively, or perhaps even maliciously. Without excusing such behavior, you can be sure of this: *isolated antagonistic behaviors do not make an antagonist.*
What is missing, among other things, is that *insatiable*
quality that drags problems out interminably.

Antagonism is conflict, a very specific kind of unhealthy conflict. Not all conflict is unhealthy, however, as
you will see in the next chapter.

Levels of Church Conflict

*C*ONFLICT is a fact of life throughout society, including the church. Conflict that hones the edge of an organization and keeps it mindful of and true to its purposes is healthy. An organization with no conflict at all (and I don't know of one) must have either no purpose at all or, at best, a very frivolous purpose.

Conflict as such is not necessarily a problem, and is not the subject of this book. On a values scale, conflict is neutral. It can be good or bad, healthy or unhealthy, creative or destructive. This book does not intend to suggest that anytime conflict emerges it means there is an antagonist somewhere at the bottom of it. In fact, *antagonism makes up only a small percentage of the wide range of conflict that exists in congregations.*

Conflict resolution techniques have been adequately presented by others, and a review of the extensive literature on that subject is beyond the scope of this book. However, aspects of conflict resolution will be discussed where they relate to the particular topic of antagonism.

Some specialists in the field of conflict resolution are now discovering that they have treated conflict too narrowly. Too often it was assumed that all parties involved in conflicts were mentally healthy, morally responsible, rational, and willing to compromise. Experience has shown that such assumptions, while applying to the great majority of individuals, overlook a very notable, vocal, and disruptive minority. The result has been to equip mentally sound and morally responsible individuals to work through healthy conflict with other mentally sound and morally responsible people, but to leave them at a loss when confronted with antagonists.

Recent literature in the area of conflict resolution has begun to recognize that there are individuals who initiate and thrive on unhealthy conflict, persons who have no desire whatsoever to see conflict resolved. Speed Leas noted that much of the existing literature on conflict does little to help people determine the severity of conflict and adjust their responses accordingly (Speed Leas, *Moving Your Church through Conflict,* Washington, D.C.: The Alban Institute, 1985). In answer to this need, Leas distinguished five levels of conflict in congregations (see Figure 1, page 33).

According to Leas, what differentiates the various levels are the *objectives* of those involved and their *use of language.*

The objective of those operating at Level I, *Problems to Solve,* is to work out a solution to the problem, whatever it is. Anger may surface (as on any level), but the focus remains on finding an amicable resolution to the conflict. Those operating at this level do not perceive the conflict as person-oriented. Full use is made of rational opportunities to work out a solution, and communication is quite open. Individuals operating on this level use language that is straightforward and centered in the here and now. They have no hidden agendas.

At Level II, *Disagreements,* the objective becomes colored with a need for self-protection. There is a shift from

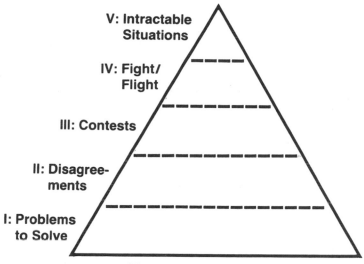

Figure 1: Levels of Conflict

unreserved openness to some guardedness (not actually hostile, except perhaps in the appearance of sarcastic overtones in the language used). At this level, individuals move away from dealing with specifics and tend toward generalizations. Those operating at Level II frequently turn to compromise as a method of dealing with differences.

Those operating at Level III, *Contests,* view conflict from a "win/lose" perspective. The objective is no longer to solve the problem. Even self-protection has faded into the background. What matters is winning, putting one's opponents "in their proper place." The language used by those operating on this level reveals some perceptual distortion. Although it occurs infrequently, healthy resolution of conflict at this level is still possible.

Parties operating at Level IV, *Fight/Flight,* have the objective of hurting their opponents in some way, getting rid of them, or both. The good of the organization is not a concern at this level. Being right and punishing those who are wrong predominates. The language used appeals to generalized and personalized principles (such as truth, freedom, and justice) and avoids the specific issue or issues at hand. At this level, the choices have crystallized into two: fighting or fleeing.

Leas described Level V, *Intractable Situations,* as "conflict run amok." Whereas the objective at Level IV is to punish or get the other out of the organization, the objective of individuals in conflict at this fifth level is purely and simply to destroy opponents, irrespective of cost to self or others.

Regarding these five levels, Leas commented: "The first two levels are easy to work with; the third is tough; the fourth and fifth are very difficult and impossible" (Speed Leas, "When Conflict Erupts in Your Church: Interview with Speed B. Leas," *Alban Institute Action Information,* vol. 9, no. 5 [1985]:16). In other words, conflict at Levels I and II, and sometimes in Level III, can often be handled by normal conflict resolution techniques and can end up being healthy. Most conflict at Level III and higher levels cannot.

Leas added that while it *might* be the case that the individuals involved in the same conflict are operating on the same level, this is not true all the time. For example, one person may enter into a conflict with the best of intentions, operating on Level I, *Problems to Solve,* and attempt to use the techniques particularly suited to that level. The other party, however, may be operating at Level IV. In such a situation the first individual, who is attempting to use techniques appropriate to Level I, will suddenly be overwhelmed. The situation could be compared to the differences between dealing with a house cat vs. a tiger. In conflict situations it is of paramount importance to recognize the type of individual you are dealing with.

In that regard, one finds that superimposing the three types of antagonists (presented earlier) onto Leas's model yields some interesting results (see Figure 2).

As the modified model in Figure 2 shows, the bulk of church conflict takes place at healthy, normal levels. The normal techniques of conflict resolution are successful in dealing with conflict at the first two levels, and to a limited extent with conflict at the third. The model in Figure 2 also indicates that hard-core antagonists may be found operating at Levels III, IV, and V, major antagonists mainly at Levels III and IV, and moderate antagonists for the most part at Level III.

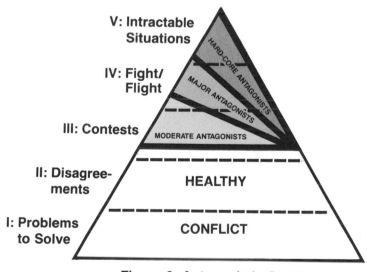

Figure 2: Antagonistic Conflict

There is one qualifying point. On matters outside an antagonist's particular area of obsession, he or she may well operate on the first two levels. For example, an antagonist may be amenable to amicable resolution of such minor conflicts as where the church picnic should be held. *May* be amenable. An antagonist may also find such a decision just the cleavage point at which to begin splitting a congregation.

Healthy resolution of church conflict requires that those involved value one another as human beings, put forth the effort required to understand opposing points of view, and mutually agree that the good of the congregation is paramount. Unfortunately, antagonists do none of these consistently. Antagonists are malevolent in intent, and therefore fall into that category of people whom M. Scott Peck designates as being evil:

> I have learned nothing in twenty years that would suggest that evil people can be rapidly influenced by any means other than raw power. They do not respond, at least in the short run, to either gentle kindness or any form of spiritual persuasion with which I am familiar. (M. Scott Peck, *People of the Lie: The Hope For Healing Human Evil,* New York: Simon and Schuster, 1983, p. 68.)

In antagonistic conflict, the use of techniques appropriate to Level I or Level II conflicts will not work, regardless of how skillfully and creatively they are applied. This book is a resource for dealing specifically with those who engage in conflict on Levels III, IV, and V.

Why Antagonism Happens in Congregations

ANTAGONISM surfaces in congregations because of:
- the nature of antagonists;
- the support antagonists receive from others; and
- the structure of congregations.

In this chapter we will look at each of these factors in turn.

The Nature of Antagonists

Antagonism exists not only in the church, but also in every type of organization and institution: in business and industry, universities, health care organizations, sports, the media, and so on. Why does antagonism exist in congregations? One reason is that it exists everywhere.

Antagonists are antagonistic by nature. If they were not antagonistic in your congregation, they would be antagonistic at another one. It is their personality. You might wistfully ask, "Why is so-and-so antagonistic?" The simple (if circular) answer is, "Because he or she is an antagonist."

Antagonists frequently exhibit the psychological defense mechanism known as *displacement,* in which the focus of behaviors is shifted to someone other than the individual who first elicited them. The behaviors are displaced because the subject—in this case the antagonist—finds it difficult (for various reasons) to direct them toward the original object.

The classic example that has been used to illustrate displacement starts with a man being reprimanded by his boss. He comes home and yells at his wife. She in turn shouts at the children. The children kick the dog. The dog chases and bites the cat. The cat claws the living room sofa.

Church antagonists displace their angry and hostile behaviors onto people in the congregation who too often are easy, available, vulnerable targets. The targets are not the cause of the antagonism, but merely recipients of it.

Support from Others

Antagonists tend to attract followers. It is the assistance of these followers that accounts in part for the escalation of antagonistic conflict in congregations from teapot tempests to the level of devastating typhoons. Here are some reasons why individuals follow antagonists:

- People sometimes mistake antagonists for activists.
- The truth is often far less exciting than lies and half-truths.
- Bad news is more exciting than good news.
- Some people are gullible, and antagonists take advantage of that.
- Some people tend to follow orders without question.
- Some people are intimidated by antagonists.
- Many persons just don't want to rock the boat.
- People follow antagonists to be one of the crowd.
- Some join antagonists as a way to express their own feelings.

- Others follow antagonists because of misguided loyalties.
- Some follow antagonists because antagonists frequently make their followers feel important.

In some ways, followers of antagonists resemble the "moderate antagonists" described in Chapter 2. Most people have a tendency to follow powerful leaders, but those who actively support antagonists allow this tendency to blind them.

The Structure of Congregations

For too long, congregations have been places where antagonists can operate with success. Their behavior is not as successful in many other areas of life because in those areas it is simply not tolerated. Antagonists have an uncanny ability to find power voids, which they subsequently rush to fill. They find that the risks are relatively small, and there are few repercussions because no one believes that they have the right to stop them.

Why has there been antagonism in churches? Because too often people have felt that antagonists had to be placated.

Because congregations are often relatively small, they are ideal places for antagonists to gain the attention they crave. Congregations in the United States consist of an average of 125 members. It is an axiom that the smaller an organization is, the more vulnerable it is to attack. The smaller the arena, the more prominent are the individuals in it. And so it is that in the small and friendly fishbowl of a congregation, antagonists more easily fill their need for attention—the need to be "big fish." Larger congregations, also, strive to create a sense of "family." That family feeling can be readily abused by antagonists. Smaller boards, committees, and other groups then frequently become the places where antagonists get their start.

Another reason why antagonists exist in congregations is that religion is an emotionally charged subject.

People typically surround the most meaningful and worthwhile areas of their lives with tripwires and alarms. Religion is one such area. The great sensitivity with which people regard their faith can be a blessing; they are guarding their treasure. But oversensitive safeguards can also be a curse, because both butterflies and thieves stand an equal chance of setting off the alarm.

Tensions over doctrinal points and practical issues can be healthy and will be part of church life until Christ returns. However, when someone with antagonistic tendencies takes hold of such issues, the result is often destructive and divisive. The antagonist is usually not interested in the issues themselves; they are only a means to his or her own peculiar end.

Why is there antagonism in congregations? Because it is here that issues of all sorts are openly prayed about, preached about, studied, and discussed.

A Biblical Perspective

*M*ARTIN LUTHER said, "The Bible is alive, it speaks to me; it has hands, it lays hold on me." Scripture has been variously described as "the manger in which the Christ-child lies," "God's love letter to the world," and "the fountain of pure wisdom." The Bible speaks of its own function in 2 Timothy 3:16: "All scripture is inspired by God and profitable for teaching, for reproof, for correction, and for training in righteousness." In this chapter we will look at what the Scriptures teach us about antagonism in the church.

Antagonism and Its Causes

The Bible speaks:

For we are not contending against flesh and blood, but against the principalities, against the powers, against the world rulers of this present darkness, against the spiritual hosts of wickedness in the heavenly places (Eph. 6:12).

The spiritual forces that stand in rebellion against God and God's claim on people lie behind (indeed, precipitate) the behavior of antagonistic individuals. C. S. Lewis humorously portrayed the reality of the demonic in *The Screwtape Letters,* and M. Scott Peck's *People of the Lie* is a profound probing of the phenomenon of human evil by a contemporary writer.

It's ironic. In spite of all the atrocities and mass murders committed in this century, the church still hasn't fully caught on to the reality of evil. In a day when many psychologists and other scientists are ready to acknowledge the frightening reality of suprahuman evil forces, the church all too often misses the boat.

When confronting an antagonist, it must be kept in mind that antagonists play into the hands of forces that are intent upon destroying the healing and caring mission of the church. One dare not sit back and watch antagonists cripple and disfigure a congregational body. The fruit of the Spirit (Gal. 5:22-23) ought to characterize the life of a Christian community, but antagonists sow the seeds of bitterness, anger, and hatred. These do not come from the Spirit but rather from the Enemy.

The Bible speaks:

> For I know that nothing good dwells within me, that is, in my flesh (Rom. 7:18).

Deep within every daughter of Eve and son of Adam lurks the desire to be one's own god, intense and burning like a hidden coal. That desire—part of fallen human nature that the apostle Paul called "the flesh"—can suddenly flare up and then, just as quickly, die away to a glowing ember. Antagonists, however, tend this fire and nourish it regularly by brooding on past injuries, present suspicions, and future insecurities. What matters most to antagonists is not forgiveness, but getting the upper hand, getting even.

The tragedy is that not only are antagonists in the grip of evil forces, they also enjoy it! What the suprahuman forces of darkness plant, the antagonist's sinful human nature incubates and brings to hideous birth.

The Bible speaks:

They are of the world, therefore what they say is of the world, and the world listens to them. We are of God. Whoever knows God listens to us, and he who is not of God does not listen to us. By this we know the spirit of truth and the spirit of error (1 John 4:5-6).

The letter of 1 John is filled with pleas to beware of "the world." John wrote, "If anyone loves the world, love for the Father is not in him" (1 John 2:15). "The world" refers to that powerful amalgamation of sinful human natures that tries to lead us away from God and attempts to make us conform to its own rules and whims and fads.

When the church acts properly as the church, it has no use for the desire to conform to what everyone else is doing. As J. B. Phillips translated Rom. 12:2—"Don't let the world around you squeeze you into its own mold, but let God re-make you so that your whole attitude of mind is changed." An antagonist is someone who delights in what the apostle Paul described as the world's mold, namely arguing, fighting, backbiting, slander, and hatred. Because an antagonist refuses to participate in church life as a repentant and forgiven sinner and insists on the way of hatred and strife, his or her presence means trouble for a congregation.

The Bible speaks:

But the serpent said to the woman, "You will not die. For God knows that when you eat of it your eyes will be opened, and you will be like God, knowing good and evil" (Gen. 3:4-5).

Genesis 3 relates the story of how human beings fell into the vise-grip of the demonic, the flesh, and the world by trying to grasp what belonged to God alone: the knowledge of good and evil. With a kind of distorted truth that similarly marks an antagonist, the serpent had promised, "You will be like God." In part, the serpent was right. But instead of being able to enjoy their newfound "independence" from God's guidance, people instead found themselves desperately separated from God, cut off from the source of life.

All humanity experiences this separation from God, as Paul asserted: " ... since all have sinned and fall short of the glory of God" (Rom. 3:23). But it is from slavery to sin that Jesus' death frees us: "So if the Son makes you free, you will be free indeed" (John 8:36); " ... in Christ God was reconciling the world to himself" (2 Cor. 5:19). Antagonists, however, steadfastly reject freedom from the slavery of sin, rejoicing in and thriving on the potential for sowing disharmony. Antagonists resist Jesus Christ and the freedom he would give them. But if Christ is the center, and the throne of the universe is the cross, then self-willed fighting and animosity have been defeated and will someday come to an end.

Antagonism and Its Effects

The Bible speaks:

By this all men will know that you are my disciples, if you have love for one another (John 13:35).

When a congregation is wracked by arguing and antagonism, its witness to the God of love is destroyed. The story is told about the apostle John that when he was very old and was carried in to speak to the congregation, he repeated one sentence over and over in a frail voice: "Little children, love one another!" That is the kind of Christianity that turned the world upside down! The message we learn from the world is that love is conditional: "I will love you *if. . . .*" But *unconditional* love is the Christian's powerful gift and witness.

Antagonists choose not to live out of the love of Christ. Strife is introduced in love's place, and with strife go jealousy and anger. Visible expressions of the unconditional love of Christ are among the first casualties of active antagonism. The reaction of some Christians to antagonists is to make excuses for them: "Oh, they think they are being loving. They're just misguided." For hard-core antagonists, and probably for major antagonists as well, this is a mistaken notion. Antagonists at these levels are evil in both intention and effect.

The Bible speaks:

> Avoid such godless chatter, for it will lead people into more and more ungodliness, and their talk will eat its way like gangrene (2 Tim. 2:16-17).

The strife and dissension caused by antagonists eat their way into the body of the local congregation. The image of gangrene is repulsive, but it is accurate nevertheless. What begins as an isolated problem has the potential to spread rapidly, endangering the very life of the entire body. Do not be deceived: antagonism can so thoroughly eat its way through a congregation that there remains only a deadly mockery of what was once a healthy, lively Christian organism.

The Bible speaks:

Do you not know that you are God's temple and that God's Spirit dwells in you? If any one destroys God's temple, God will destroy him. For God's temple is holy, and that temple you are (1 Cor. 3:16-17).

Here Paul warned the Corinthians that God does not tolerate any destructive activity in his temple. And what is God's temple? Not a building, but the congregation itself, for the congregation is the body of God's own Son. To defile that body, as antagonism does, kindles God's wrath. Ultimately, God threatens to destroy the destroyers of his temple.

What is the effect of antagonism on God's people? The effect that surpasses all others is destruction. Antagonism destroys the unique, loving witness of Christian individuals and the vitality of the congregation, calling forth God's anger.

Treatment for Antagonism

The Bible speaks:

I appeal to you, brethren, to take note of those who create dissensions and difficulties, in opposition to the doctrine which you have been taught; avoid them (Rom. 16:17).

The apostle Paul pleaded with the leaders of the Christians at Rome to "take note of" antagonists in the congregation. This is always the first step toward dealing with antagonism: take note of it, be aware of it, watch out for it. Paul did not leave to his readers' imaginations exactly whom it was they were to take note of. They were to watch out for those who created dissension and caused divisions. To be aware of and make special note of individuals you see causing strife in a congregation is indeed what the Lord, through the apostle, urges you to do.

The Bible speaks:

... so be wise as serpents and innocent as doves (Matt. 10:16).

It is the Lord who spoke these words to his apostles before sending them out "as sheep in the midst of wolves" (v. 16). Here the Lord gave his sheep a mandate to possess and to use wisdom. Paul wrote of Satan, "For we are not ignorant of his designs" (2 Cor. 2:11). Christians are called to be wise in the ways of antagonism. You, the sheep, have been given a mandate to deal with wolves.

The Bible speaks:

For such men are false apostles, deceitful workmen, disguising themselves as apostles of Christ. And no wonder, for even Satan disguises himself as an angel of light (2 Cor. 11:13-14).

The Bible tells the truth, even when the truth might be uncomfortable. In this passage Paul exposed individuals who were claiming to do the same work he was doing. Paul saw clearly, and what he saw he named accurately. Jesus did so as well when he said, "You serpents, you brood of vipers," (Matt. 23:33).

I sincerely doubt that either Paul or Jesus enjoyed throwing the hot, white light of truth on their opponents. I always picture Jesus speaking these necessary words with great pain. The point, however, is that the one place antagonism cannot live or grow is under the bright light of truth.

The Bible doesn't say that bringing antagonism to light is easy. It's risky. But it is a risk that church leaders and church members must take. What an absurd tragedy for the flock to be devoured because everyone thought it impolite to cry, "Wolf!"

The Bible speaks:

If your brother sins against you, go and tell him his fault, between you and him alone. If he listens to you, you have gained your brother. But if he does not listen, take one or two others along with you, that every word may be confirmed by the evidence of two or three witnesses. If he refuses to listen to them, tell it to the church; and if he refuses even to listen to the church, let him be to you as a Gentile and a tax collector (Matt. 18:15-17).

The words of Christ in this passage are the basis for many churches' procedures for discipline of members. The steps laid out here are clear, but must be used with great caution.
1. Confront the individual privately first.
2. Confront him or her in the company of one or two witnesses.
3. Bring him or her before the congregation's governing body.

When used correctly, this system as Christ established it can be a very firm, caring, and loving way to handle individuals who are persistent troublemakers in a congregation. The aim is always to reclaim one who continually chooses to reject God's love, for the good of that person and the good of the Christian community.

As you are going through this process, though, you need to be aware of the manipulative power of antagonists. Antagonists are all too adept at turning the tables, and there are many instances where a formal first-stage Matthew 18 admonition was used by an antagonist as an occasion to assail the one beginning the process. This was further compounded when the injured party returned with two others, as directed by step two of the process, and the antagonist proceeded to make an alliance with them against the first individual.

The guidelines in Matthew 18 should not be a prescription for exposing oneself and the congregation to further harm. They are firm, highly principled, and graduated procedures for attempting to bring an erring brother or sister back into the compass of love that is the Christian community. By the time matters have reached a point where the principles of Matthew 18 are invoked, the actors in the drama each have their clearly defined roles: there is one who is the recipient of discipline and one who is the administrant. Use these principles as they were intended.

The Bible speaks:

> Then Peter came up and said to him, "Lord, how often shall my brother sin against me, and I forgive him? As many as seven times?" Jesus said to him, "I do not say to you seven times, but seventy times seven" (Matt. 18:21-22).

Forgiveness and strong, confrontive actions are by no means mutually exclusive. This passage in which Jesus replied to Peter's question immediately follows the passage in which the Lord instructed his disciples what disciplinary actions to take. There is no limit to the forgiveness you offer an antagonist, just as God puts no limit on the number of times he will forgive. In this passage Jesus called Peter—just as he calls you and me—to an imitation of God's forgiving nature. Jesus' forgiveness is valid, ready, and waiting for all who do not reject it. So also should be the forgiveness of Jesus' followers. The question of whether or not to forgive need never be raised among God's children. It is a given.

Forgiveness is not license for an antagonist to continue behavior injurious to the welfare of the church, however, nor is it an escape from the clear principles of discipline laid out in Matthew 18:15-17. That discipline is called into action when someone continues to sin, and it moves forward inexorably if the person does not cease.

When the dynamic combination of repentance and forgiveness is in effect, it results in the healing of a relationship that had been broken. An antagonist's repentance and acceptance of forgiveness is of great moment both on earth and in heaven. It is something earnestly to hope and pray for; not so that you can boast about your forgiving nature, but so that the relationship can be healed. The grim fact, however, is that most antagonists neither expect nor want forgiveness. They are simply not interested in the healing that forgiveness can bring.

When dealing with an antagonist, by all means follow the prescriptions of Matthew 18:15-17 and 21-22. But remember Titus 3:10-11 (see below) as well.

The Bible speaks:

> As for a man who is factious, after admonishing him once or twice, have nothing more to do with him, knowing that such a person is perverted and sinful; he is self-condemned (Titus 3:10-11).

Saving this passage for last was a deliberate choice. Dismissing someone should not be lightly done. The words "have nothing more to do with him" are a clear-cut response to an individual who persists in divisiveness after the first and second warnings. *Factious* has the same root as the word *faction,* and here describes someone who sets up warring parties in a church. Paul addressed Titus as the leader of the congregation in Cyprus. Titus was not to engage in extensive attempts to smooth things over with the troublemaker; he was simply to avoid that person.

The apostolic guideline is clear: when confronted with an antagonist, face the *probability* that change simply will not occur. He or she is "self-condemned," in Paul's words. Stay away from that person as best you can—emotionally and physically.

Antagonists are not new phenomena. The Bible speaks straightforwardly about their existence, their motivations, their effects, and the necessary treatment. These verses and admonitions do not exist in a vacuum; they are part of God's total message of Scripture. They are alive. They lay hold of you and me. We struggle with them. We wrestle. And we accept and follow our Lord's guidance as best we can.

A Question of Values

*B*EFORE you stands an antagonist—subtle and menacing as a wolf. Around you is the congregation—confused and frightened as a flock of sheep. What do you do? Doing nothing concedes the antagonist's right to continue behaving destructively, damaging God's people and discrediting God's mission. Taking decisive action, however, is risky. Ethical questions—values-charged questions—are reviewed again and again: *What kind of Christian am I? How can I justify my actions to myself? How can I legitimately call someone an antagonist? Isn't that judgmental? As a Christian, shouldn't I seek to minister to the antagonist?*

First of all, there can be no doubt that Christians are called to minister to all people. Christians are called to pray for their enemies, to bless those who curse them, to love the loveless. A Christian is to minister to an antagonist no less than to a saint, for Jesus Christ has given his life for both.

The dilemma arises when trying to figure out how to minister to, how to bless, and how to love an antagonist. Surely, antagonists are not loved or blessed simply by letting them have their own way. Common sense tells us that. Letting a small child play with matches or permitting a drunk person to drive a car are most *unloving* actions. Similarly, allowing antagonists to wreak havoc in the midst and at the expense of God's people is not loving antagonists or others.

There is also the risk that the very ones you are trying to help may misunderstand you. How will the sheep view a shepherd who assertively confronts a wolf—especially if that wolf happens to be wearing sheep's clothing? Perhaps unaware that they have been spared, the sheep might misconstrue the actions of the shepherd. "Oh, I guess that shepherd doesn't really believe much in love and forgiveness after all!" they murmur to one another. Like it or not, the spotlight is on you—from within and without. What do you do?

There is no ducking the question about judgment. "Judge not, that you be not judged," Jesus said (Matt. 7:1). Identifying someone as an antagonist is clearly a judgment. But in Matthew 7 Jesus was issuing a warning against judgmentalism, not judgments. One ought not predict the ultimate destiny of an antagonist, but you certainly should use your powers of discernment to identify someone who is causing division in the body of Christ. Christians (and everyone else) must make judgments all the time—frequently in matters laden with values. Dealing with antagonists is just one of the areas in life where you need to take a close, accurate look and name what you see for what it is before you arrive at an appropriate course of action.

When confronted with an antagonist, you will have to make a choice as to how to deal with that individual. You will deal with the antagonist one way or another:
- You can bury your head in the sand.
- You can take a wait-and-see stance, saying in effect, "If one more sheep is lost, *then* we'll do something about it."
- You can take definitive action to solve the problem.

Deciding how to deal with antagonists is difficult. Typically there is no perfect solution, so it becomes a matter of deciding how best to deal with them. Your decision will require some deep soul-searching and prayerful consideration, for this is a weighty matter—not one to be entered into lightly.

Realizing that your actions will have painful side-effects may cause guilt feelings. You may lament, "If I can't deal with an antagonist without hurting him or her, then I won't do anything at all." When you realize however, that whatever you do in dealing with antagonists will result in pain, some of your guilt may be alleviated. Even so, you may never be entirely comfortable with your decision. This is as it should be. It indicates that you are a caring human being who hurts when a fellow human being hurts. But painful decisions are part of life.

How do you deal with antagonists? What is the caring, loving, and fair course to take? Here is a key that may help when you struggle with difficult ethical decisions. Do not "turn the other cheek" or "forgive seventy times seven" to escape from an uncomfortable situation. Using such passages out of fear is not being true to the sense of those passages.

Fear is a natural and realistic reaction to antagonists. An antagonist can strike back like a rattlesnake. It often seems easier to avoid them, using whatever rationale (theological or otherwise) you can dredge up. "Turning" and "forgiving" should be done when it is the Christian thing to do, not simply because it might make things easier for you. "Forgiveness" flowing from fear of retribution or distaste for conflict is a sham. Expediency is not forgiveness. Turning the other cheek and letting the antagonist continue to behave disruptively is the wide and easy road "that leads to destruction" (Matt. 7:13).

You also may have heard the common argument that an individual has done so much good that his or her antagonism should therefore be overlooked. The same argument was advanced in support of Mussolini and Hitler in the 1930s. "At least the trains run on time" was a common apology offered for Mussolini's excesses. When a Berlin family vanished in the middle of the night, the next morning a neighbor at the breakfast table might say, "The Führer has gone too far—." Before the statement was finished, someone else would break in saying, "Quiet! Just remember what it was like before God gave us the Führer. No jobs, no security, no food. Be still and eat."

You cannot and should not deal with antagonists solely on the basis of the good they might do. Only the historically blind would deny that Hitler helped Germany in some ways, playing a major part in a startling economic recovery from the pits of depression. History penned by the victors makes a totally negative view of Hitler seem obvious today, but amid the daily routines of life at that time, matters were far less clear.

The tragedy of the People's Temple in Guyana led by the Reverend Jim Jones is an example of unchecked antagonism in the name of religion. Jones accomplished some worthwhile things for poor people early in his ministry, both in Indianapolis and subsequently in San Francisco. He became a celebrity, appearing with such notables as Dianne Feinstein, the mayor of San Francisco, and Rosalynn Carter, the wife of the president of the United States. People assumed he was an activist. Too few questioned his methods. Congressman Leo Ryan was one who did. When the commune moved to Guyana and the terrible mass homicide/suicide occurred, Congressman Ryan and others were swept away as sacrificial lambs along with the rest. The unsuccessful attempt to deal with this antagonist came too late, was inadequate, and involved too few.

These tragic historical examples demonstrate the serious nature of the problem. Dealing with antagonists is never easy. No matter what is done, someone will feel pain, be it the antagonist, the congregation, or yourself. But bear in mind that the right kind of pain can also be a precursor of healing.

Part Two

A GUIDE FOR IDENTIFYING ANTAGONISTS

Personality Characteristics of Antagonists

*D*ISTINGUISHING those who are true antagonists from those who are not is essential. Otherwise there is a serious risk of misjudging the actual level of conflict confronting you. You can begin to identify antagonists by measuring individuals you might have questions about against the definition you first read in Chapter 1:

> Antagonists are individuals who, on the basis of nonsubstantive evidence, go out of their way to make insatiable demands, usually attacking the person or performance of others. These attacks are selfish in nature, tearing down rather than building up, and are frequently directed against those in a leadership capacity.

Next, ask yourself the following questions about the individual:

1. Is his or her behavior disruptive?
2. Is the attack irrational?

3. Does the person go out of the way to initiate trouble?
4. Are the person's demands insatiable?
5. Are the concerns upon which he or she bases the attack minimal or fabricated?
6. Does the person avoid causes that involve personal risk, suffering, or sacrifice?
7. Does the person's motivation appear selfish?

If the answers to several of these questions are yes, that is enough to suggest that a person might be an antagonist. Even if the answers to a few are no, you need to take a closer look.

As you read this chapter, be aware of two pitfalls. One is expecting to find a cookbook-style description of an antagonistic personality. There is no such thing. Antagonists are not "always this, plus a little of this, and a little bit of that." A second pitfall is to carelessly prejudge others, dehumanizing them as mere categories for identification.

Despite these dangers in trying to identify antagonists, it is still true that antagonists tend to display distinctive combinations of clustered personality traits and psychiatric syndromes. This commonality is enough to justify the following discussion. But exercise your good judgment when you evaluate others. People should never be treated as objects, carelessly labeled and then discarded.

To understand the mental and emotional workings of antagonists, you need to understand both their general personality tendencies and also their characteristic psychiatric syndromes.

General Personality Characteristics

Antagonists frequently evidence at least several of five personality characteristics: negative self-concept, narcissism, aggression, rigidity, and authoritarianism. Although these same personality traits occur in "normal" individuals as well, two factors distinguish these characteristics as they appear in antagonists: first, antagonists usually display at least several of them; second, antagonists exhibit them in extreme forms.

Negative self-concept. Self-image or self-concept is psychological shorthand for the feelings and thoughts, conscious and unconscious, that an individual has about himself or herself. Self-concept is an important factor in how people experience life. If one's self-concept is positive, society and other people tend to appear appealing, good, inviting, or exciting, but if one's self-concept is negative, the world appears frightening, angry, hostile, and threatening. A positive self-concept opens the door to regarding others positively, enables meaningful social interaction, and leads to productive behaviors. A negative self-concept often creates difficulty in properly understanding or relating to others. An individual with a negative self-concept frequently views the world with excessive pessimism.

Many people who are not antagonists struggle with low self-image. However, most individuals with this problem tend to react by withdrawing from others. Antagonists, on the other hand, try to build themselves up by tearing others down. They express their inner struggles with a negative self-concept by attacking people, enjoying the failures and misfortunes of others while they project their own sense of worthlessness onto them.

Narcissism. Narcissism is a personality pattern in which a person displays an excessive sense of self-importance and preoccupation with eliciting the admiration and attention of others. Superficially, the root problem of a narcissistic individual seems to lie in an overdose of positive self-concept, but appearances are deceiving. More often than not, narcissism disguises an inner sense of inadequacy. To compensate for these negative feelings—that is, to cover them up—a narcissistic individual greedily fishes for and hungrily devours the praise and attention of others. Yet attempting to hide feelings of inferiority and worthlessness in this way rarely works. The "praise-or-attention-fix" lasts only a short time, and the individual is compelled to solicit attention and admiration with the intensity and desperation of a chemically-dependent person. Narcissistic people desperately need care, but unfortunately, they are usually incapable of either receiving or benefiting from it.

Narcissistic people also find difficulty respecting the rights and feelings of others—to the extent of obliviousness to them—but other individuals may be slow to perceive narcissistic antagonists as self-centered. Skilled in the art of deception, narcissistic antagonists are adept at appearing interested in others to win popularity. Their efforts are focused on feeding their own egos, however, and they are unable to meet even the most basic needs of others. There is little authentic, personal interaction; others are treated as means to fulfill the need for affirmation.

Narcissistic individuals who are antagonists are extremely reluctant to admit wrongdoing. They cannot conceive of being in error, because "right" is what meets their needs, and "wrong" is what obstructs the meeting of those needs. According to these self-gratifying standards, the person chairing a church meeting who denies an antagonist's purpose by calling a halt to an uninvited tirade is judged by the antagonist as inherently wrong. Since the antagonist defines the world so that he or she is never wrong, others are always assumed to be at fault.

Aggression. Antagonists also display patterns of aggressive behavior that permeate their entire personalities. Angry at self, the world, and any convenient situation or person, antagonists seem to wander through life seeking, inviting, and collecting injustices against themselves. Every perceived or actual wrong they experience is stored in their memories and periodically replayed to supply fuel for their anger.

Everyone has aggressive feelings at times, but for antagonists, aggression is a way of life. Living to "get even," they constantly brood over past injustices to stoke the fires of their wrath.

When antagonists behave aggressively, they tend to legitimize their violent outbursts by projecting those feelings onto others, convincing themselves that others are treating them unfairly. In that way, antagonists easily justify their aggressive actions in their own minds.

Not all aggression manifests itself in physical or verbal activity. In fact, passive aggression can be every bit as malicious as active aggression. Characterized by procrastination and constant inefficiency, this passive aggression is tailor-made to frustrate others. For example, a passive-aggressive antagonist serving on a board might constantly obstruct normal procedure by means of delay tactics or otherwise misusing the bylaws. A passive-aggressive antagonist undertaking an assignment for a committee will have plenty of excuses, but won't have the work in hand when the deadline arrives. Using all available means, the passive-aggressive person sets roadblock after roadblock in silent acts of aggression.

Rigidity. When emotional and personal growth stops too soon, rigidity is one result. Rigidity is characterized by inflexibility of thought, usually coupled with excessive concern for precise and accurate procedure (as defined by the rigid individual). Someone with a rigid personality sees the world as totally static; his or her explanation of events is, by definition, the unquestionably correct interpretation. Rigid individuals ridicule or ignore differing opinions and skillfully overlook contrary evidence. Attempting to create a sense of security in an apparently unstable, frightening world, those who have rigid personality structures are devoted to keeping their narrow views intact.

Antagonists with rigid personality structures are prone to antagonistic behaviors for two reasons: (1) Their feelings of peace, security, and harmony are heavily dependent on the integrity of their world views. When it becomes impossible for them to ignore dissent, they strike out against those who threaten to topple their systems. (2) They are especially jealous of leaders, because people in authority have the power to inject disturbing input. Therefore, rigid antagonists frequently employ their simplistic rules and regulations as weapons against leaders.

Authoritarianism. Authoritarian individuals are characterized by two seemingly contradictory drives: (1) the need to admire and submit to those considered "powerful"; and (2) the need to be in authority and make others submit to them. Individuals with authoritarian tendencies divide the world into two camps: those who are "strong" and those who are "weak." Whatever is designated as strong elicits the authoritarian's veneration (usually involving a combination of fear and admiration) and a desire to submit to the stronger object. Whatever is characterized as weak arouses a desire to dominate, attack, and humiliate or annihilate the weaker object. This is why stronger individuals are more immune to antagonists than weaker individuals.

Psychiatric Syndromes

In addition to manifesting an excess of the above personality characteristics, antagonists commonly possess one or both of two clinical syndromes: *paranoid personality* and *antisocial personality.* The five general personality characteristics can combine with either one or both of these.

Paranoid personality. Paranoid-related attitudes and activities encompass a wide range—from minor suspicion present in everyone at one time or another to severe, paranoid schizophrenia found in a few individuals. Most antagonists fall into the middle and upper portions of the paranoid spectrum. Marks of a paranoid personality include persistent, unwarranted guardedness and mistrust of others; delusions of grandeur; lack of genuine emotions; and hypersensitivity. Because they distrust others, paranoid persons try to find hidden meanings in words and actions, continually looking for ulterior motives behind what others say.

Many paranoid persons are capable of functioning in society, maintaining contact with reality except in areas bordering on their delusions. Despite their adequate handling of daily activities, they commonly experience difficulty in relating to others; disagreements and arguments are commonplace. Paranoid individuals find coworkers and authority figures most difficult to get along with.

Stemming from their mistrust of others, paranoid persons rarely seek counseling or psychotherapy. Furthermore, they would interpret a gentle and loving suggestion to seek professional help as a vicious attack, serving only to validate the notion that others are out to get them. When they are forced to obtain therapeutic help, results are usually negligible. Convinced that the therapist is in collaboration with others against them, the paranoid usually cannot trust the therapist sufficiently to open up and receive help.

Along with delusions of persecution, paranoid antagonists also have delusions of grandeur, seeing themselves as centers of attention. They believe in the "revolution of the universe around the perpendicular pronoun," making it easy for them to believe that others—especially others in leadership positions—are plotting against them.

A paranoid person often projects his or her own feelings onto others. If, in a social gathering, a leader accidentally forgets to shake a paranoid antagonist's hand, the paranoid might blow the incident out of all proportion in his or her own mind. The wrath carried inside the antagonist will be attributed by mental sleight of hand to the leader, as if the leader were angry with the antagonist. By unconsciously projecting his or her negative feelings, the paranoid individual begins to believe that he or she is persecuted by the leader and only acts in self-defense when he or she attacks.

A church leader is usually tempted to try using reason to convince a paranoid antagonist that his or her delusions are false, yet any attempted reasoning in this matter is quite impossible. It is precisely at that point where the individual pushes reality aside. When a nonparanoid individual is similarly engaged in rational discussion, he or she would be more likely to say, "I guess I have been acting foolishly." Not so with the paranoid antagonist; the leader will merely demonstrate that he or she is supposedly out to get the antagonist, doesn't understand, or has been misled by others.

A most alarming aspect of the paranoid delusional system is the kernel of truth it inevitably contains. This should not be so surprising; just as it is impossible for a church leader to be 100% right, it is similarly difficult for a paranoid antagonist to be 100% wrong. The danger becomes apparent when a paranoid antagonist is able to convince others that his or her entire delusion is accurate because a small bit is based on reality.

Antisocial personality. Most antagonists suffer from more than one disorder. While it is the case that antagonists often exhibit classic paranoia, a second syndrome accompanying and aggravating paranoia in many antagonists is an antisocial personality (alternatively known as psychopathy or sociopathy). People with antisocial personalities suffer from a significant lack of moral development, accompanied by an inability to live within the limits of socially acceptable behavior.

Antisocial individuals are usually very likable, especially at first; they are often bright and spontaneous. They are also manipulative and guileful, treating others as objects for accomplishing their own ends.

As a result of inadequately developed consciences, antagonists with antisocial personalities experience little guilt or anxiety over the pain they inflict on others. For example, the anguish and humiliation a church leader might experience as the antagonist attempts to force him or her out of office will not affect the antagonist. The antisocial antagonist's actions appear cruel to others, but he or she is incapable of fully understanding the moral concept *cruel.*

Antisocial antagonists are adept at putting up a good front in order to obtain the admiration and support of others. Their extreme likability enables them to put others at ease almost effortlessly.

Antisocial antagonists tend to lack the ability to learn from prior experience. Here Santayana's comment applies: "Those who cannot remember the past are condemned to repeat it." Unable to benefit from experience, antagonists are repeat offenders. Sometimes they change the location of their games, but they never stop playing them.

These individuals have difficulty maintaining in-depth relationships. To be sure, they are often popular, having many acquaintances, but they have no intimate friends. The emotions that they have are shallow and are rarely shared with others—or even acknowledged by the antagonists themselves.

When finally confronted with their own unacceptable behavior, antisocial antagonists might ardently promise to change. Indeed they might seem to change—for a while. But then the same behavior will reappear. Like paranoia, an antisocial personality is highly resistant to change. Discomfort moves the average person to seek help, but an antisocial individual experiences no discomfort. The only anxiety that person suffers is the fear of being unable to achieve his or her purposes.

This completes a basic profile of antagonistic personalities and their characteristics. You may have noted characteristics that remind you of antagonistic individuals you encountered in the past. You may also be worried by

the fact that you have identified some antagonistic characteristics in yourself or someone who is important to you.
Relax. All these traits exist to some degree in everyone.
*What distinguishes nonantagonists from antagonists is that
these characteristics do not dominate the personalities of
nonantagonists.*

Red Flags of Antagonism

ANTAGONISTS typically walk around displaying "red flags" that say (to those who recognize them), "I'm an antagonist and proud of it!" This chapter identifies some of the red flags antagonists display even before they commence an attack.

After you finish this chapter, you might find yourself looking suspiciously at your coworkers, neighbors, and friends. With paranoid zeal you may think you see antagonists under every rock and dust ruffle. Trust me: your initial, excessive suspicion will pass in due time, and you will be left with what Karl Menninger has called *healthy paranoia,* an attitude enabling you to be on your guard without being guarded, to defend yourself without being defensive.

Antagonists rarely wave only one flag. Usually an antagonist displays several—often half a dozen or more. Not all flags proclaim with equal clarity, "I am an antagonist." Some flags announce, "I might be an antagonist *if* you see more flags in my hand." To complicate matters, in a few instances persons who wave several red flags are not antagonistic at all. By and large, however, antagonists identify themselves *clearly* and do so *early.* Just pay attention to the signals.

You may react to what you read by listing exceptions you know: "So-and-so does that, but he's not an antagonist." Or perhaps, "I do that, and I'm not an antagonist." There are exceptions, of course. Still, as the park ranger warned the city slicker, "If you see a black animal with a white stripe and bushy tail, don't pet it." The presence of one or more red flags does not guarantee that you are dealing with an antagonist. But it will give you fair warning to exercise caution.

What follows is a review, in descending order of severity, of the parade of red flags antagonists often display before they go on the offensive in congregations.

The Previous Track Record Flag

Some antagonists will wave a red flag announcing: "See how antagonistically I behaved before!" They could have played the role of antagonist earlier in the present congregation, or they might have done so in another congregation. Do not ignore this clear flag or say, "It won't happen to me." The data indicates that those with antagonistic track records tend not to reform. A few might, and for that be grateful, but most simply will not. This is not to deny the power of God to work in people's hearts. As C. S. Lewis pointed out, however, there are those who persistently say to God, "*My* will be done," and God reluctantly says in the end, "Okay, your will *be* done then."

The Parallel Track Record Flag

Individuals who behave antagonistically in other arenas of life are prime candidates to become active antagonists in the church. These persons may not now behave antagonistically in the church, but do behave this way in one or more other organizations, such as the local school system, the workplace, or in a social club. He or she may even gloat about these antagonistic behaviors. In so doing, the individual conspicuously waves a red flag before you.

You might expect these people to keep silent about their antagonism lest they be detected, but antagonists can be irrational about this. Their grandiose natures cause them to believe that everyone will wholeheartedly support their activities—indeed, they are convinced that no one could possibly disagree with them.

The Nameless Others Flag

All leaders, whatever their position, receive criticism from time to time. Sometimes the criticism is valid, helpful, and legitimate. Even when the criticism is not valid, it still can indicate a healthy relationship in process—a sign of trust from the other person.

When someone offers you a word of criticism, however, and adds, "There are X number of other people who feel the same way," chances are excellent that you are talking with an antagonist. These "others" may be phantoms of the antagonist's imagination, invented to validate his or her own feelings and to threaten you. Or they may be followers of the antagonist. Whether they exist or not is immaterial, because individuals who are not antagonistic don't need to talk about "all the others" who feel the same way; they simply express *their own* thoughts and feelings.

The litmus test to determine whether someone is or is not an antagonist in this situation is to respond casually, "Oh, I'm sorry to hear that. Who are these other people?" If the person lists a few names, you are probably not faced with an antagonist. An antagonist is more likely to answer: "They came to me in the strictest of confidence."

The Predecessor-Downer Flag

Beware of those who denounce your predecessor (in whatever position you hold) and praise you at the same time. They might say something like, "You're my kind of leader, a person I can relate to—not like the others." In certain ways, everyone enjoys hearing words like these. Both pastors and lay leaders can be seduced by such compliments, but a person criticizing others and simultaneously flattering you carries a flag of blazing scarlet. Someday you may be a former leader, and those who build up the new leader will do so at your expense.

The Instant Buddy Flag

Be cautious with those who relate to you in an overly friendly fashion as soon as you move to a new congregation or immediately after they transfer into your congregation. When you first arrive, these individuals might be among the first to invite you to dinner. While you are together, antagonists will characteristically spend much time and effort probing you and trying to become intimately acquainted. Later, their inquisitiveness will turn to the proverbially cool contempt bred of familiarity.

The Gushing Praise Flag

Have you ever had someone heap excessive praise on you? That kind of positive reinforcement is nice, isn't it? But Prov. 27:21 points out that succumbing to the praise of others can be hazardous to your health:

> The crucible is for silver,
> and the furnace is for gold,
> and a man is judged by his praise.

Those who lavish effusive, gushing praise on you now will often be equally generous with their criticism later.

What causes this shift? One possibility may be unrealistic expectations. To be human is to have faults. You cannot sustain the level of perfection that antagonists expect. It is also possible that they become jealous of the image they have built up for you and consequently seek to destroy it by bringing you down to size. In any case, beware of someone who heaps excessive praise on you. This person is waving a red flag.

The "I Gotcha" Flag

Beware of those who try to catch you in error—for example, those who ask you questions when you know they already know the answers. Imagine that you just finished presenting a devotion based on a new translation of the Bible. Someone who has antagonistic tendencies might ask (knowing the answer full well), "What version of the Bible does our denomination recommend?" This kind of question is mere subterfuge—an obvious attempt to force you into an admission of error or a defensive response. The Pharisees and Sadducees attempted to entrap Jesus with similar deceitful questions. Those who display such behavior offer public warnings that they may be antagonists.

The Extraordinary Likability Flag

I'm sure you have already met an individual like this—the kind of person you immediately like, enjoy, and feel comfortable around, someone so disarmingly charming that he or she gives you no reason to withhold anything in a relationship. Someone like this, who exudes only smoothness and perfection, might be an antagonist.

Surprising? Certainly. But true nonetheless. Beware of smooth individuals who seem to have no foibles. To be sure, other red flags need to be present before one can be confident of such an individual's antagonistic leanings, but be vigilant.

The Church Hopper Flag

Beware of those who consistently move from congregation to congregation. I am not referring to people who move frequently because their occupations require them to do so. Antagonists change congregations because they are dissatisfied with the church staff, the lay leadership, or the outcome of a decision in the previous church. Indeed, they often confide that they have been dissatisfied with almost every pastor or lay leader with whom they were previously associated. At the same time, church hoppers will build you up. "Finally," they exclaim, "I have found the leader for me!" If they are indeed antagonists and you permit them to run roughshod over you, they could be right.

The Liar Flag

Beware of individuals who lie. Their lying need not be specifically associated with antagonistic activity; people who lie—about anything—tend to be more antagonistic than those who don't. Further, the lie might involve something quite harmless, such as a small detail about where one went to school or whether one served on a particular board in a former congregation. It matters not. The simple act of failing to tell the truth is a behavioral signal. A liar is someone who may be a potential antagonist.

The Aggressive Means Flag

You can sometimes recognize antagonists by the means they propose or employ to accomplish their ends. Antagonists tend to use means that are extreme, unethical, combative, or any combination of these. Vicious language that impeaches the character of another is a mark of an antagonist; careful, reasoned assertions concerning another person's stance on an issue is the mark of someone seeking to find a solution.

"Aha!" someone might say. "Then Dietrich Bonhoeffer was an antagonist because he contemplated and undertook a violent solution to the problem of Hitler." No. As I said at the beginning of the chapter, it's not as simple as that. After noticing that a particular individual uses aggressive means, one needs to ask further questions: How many other red flags are present? What are the circumstances of the situation? Only by answering these questions can you determine whether the person is truly an antagonist.

The Flashing $$$ Flag

Anyone who conspicuously uses money has better than average potential to be an antagonist. Churches are ideal places for them to demonstrate this characteristic. An antagonist is likely to make a spectacular contribution, visible to all, to fund a special program. I am not referring to those generous individuals who are inconspicuous in their giving, but rather to persons who make a public display of their generosity. As a church leader, you might be tempted to disregard the flashing $$$ flag. Face it: it is wonderful to receive donations, especially when the need is great—as is often the case. But be careful not to sell out for money. The long-term costs are too great.

The Note Taker Flag

Be wary of those who take notes at inappropriate times—such as during a coffee-hour conversation—when an off-the-cuff opinion is expressed on a sensitive issue. Inappropriate note takers are often budding antagonists.

The Portfolio Flag

Antagonists occasionally make a practice of carrying impressively stuffed portfolios to demonstrate that they possess evidence for their charges. In addition, they may start carrying these materials long before any antagonistic attack commences. Their folders often contain meaningless filler: old church bulletins, minutes of meetings dealing with unrelated issues, grocery lists, and so on—anything to use as "paper daggers" to intimidate others.

The Kentron Flag

Kentron is a New Testament Greek word meaning "something that pierces." It is translated into English as "goad" or "sting." A person who has a "kentron" possesses power associated with tyranny—not power resting on a sense of self-worth and dignity, but rather on the painful prodding of a goad (a wooden stick tipped with an iron point).

The kentron flag describes someone who uses sharp, cutting language such as sarcasm or a barbed comment disguised as a joke. An individual who consistently resorts to these tactics is a viable candidate for the position of antagonist.

The Different Drummer Flag

Beware of those who conspicuously resist established policies, insisting on doing things their own way. Here is an example: One congregation arranged for all boards to meet at the church on the first Monday night of each month so the pastor and the congregation's president could move from meeting to meeting. But the newly elected head of the evangelism board arbitrarily decided to move the meeting to her home, which made it difficult for the pastor and president to give input to that board.

A "different drummer" makes these changes independently and often by surprise, saying things like, "I've never played by the rules; I've never been a good soldier." Such a person feels compelled to march to the beat played on his or her own drum. Certainly a degree of independence is healthy, and many people having these characteristics are in no way antagonistic. An antagonist, however, follows only the rule of expediency: "Rules are good for others, not for me." This attitude can play havoc with orderly congregational life.

The Pest Flag

A "pest" may be an insatiable questioner, a persistent suggester, or an incessant caller. This is a less significant red flag; many pesky persons are not antagonists but simply well-intentioned individuals who end up being nuisances. Occasionally, however, such behavior may be the tip of the iceberg—a fairly innocent behavior that results from an antagonistic personality. People who first appear to be simply pests may later prove to be thoroughgoing antagonists.

The Cause Flag

Philip Melanchthon, the 16th-century reformer and scholar (who was intimately acquainted with the problems of writing), once said, "Nothing can be stated so perfectly as not to be misunderstood." It is for that reason that I hesitate to include this red flag. But the relevance of this flag warrants its inclusion.

I thank God for the individuals throughout history who promoted a cause and helped to right some of the world's great wrongs. Nonetheless, there appears to be a correlation between individuals who promote causes and those who behave antagonistically. Obviously, not everyone who supports a cause should be branded an antagonist, and therefore this flag should attract less attention than the others. One associated flag you might want to look for is how far someone will go to promote a cause (see the Aggressive Means Flag). Carrying a placard is not the same as setting fire to a building.

The School of Hard Knocks Flag

Successful people with little formal education or those who have struggled against great adversity to obtain a good education or to succeed are colloquially labeled "graduates of the school of hard knocks." Most graduates of this "school" are not antagonists. It is nevertheless startling to note how many antagonists have had to fight their way up. Antagonists are particularly apt to flaunt their struggle. They seem compelled to brag about it as though it somehow validates their actions. Not every self-made person is an antagonist, but be cautious when you spot this red flag along with others.

The Situational Loser Flag

Every congregation makes decisions, and decisions create sides. Occasionally, these disagreements can escalate into bitter affairs in which hurt feelings and misunderstandings run rampant.

When a conflict requires a decision, some will win and others will lose. While disagreements and conflicts can provide occasions for growth, there are some people who take losses very poorly. For them, being on the losing end of an issue precipitates outwardly antagonistic behavior.

You may want to pay a bit more attention to congregational members who lose on a particular issue, especially when the level of conflict approached that of "contest" or above as described in Chapter 3. This red flag is only significant when it appears with others.

Avoid making any snap judgments about individuals. But do remember that for the sake of the congregation, individuals in it, and God's mission and ministry, discernment is necessary.

Airport security people have behavioral profiles of bombers and terrorists. These are not infallible, but they are the best guides available for alerting security personnel to potential problems. Officials pay far more attention to the people who match the profile than to those who don't, because they know where trouble usually comes from. The same is true with antagonists. Individuals who wave these red flags merit close scrutiny. After some consideration, you may relax, or you may decide to pay close attention. Knowing these indicators—and knowing them well—is worth your time.

Warning Signs and How to Recognize Them

*J*UST as antagonists reveal themselves by their red flags, they also exhibit warning signs that telegraph their intentions to *begin an attack.* This chapter covers those warning signals—both early and late—and how to recognize them so that you can take appropriate action to minimize or prevent the attack.

Before you sound the alarm, however, you need to satisfy yourself with regard to two conditions:
- Warning signs are indeed present.
- They are coming from a person who has been waving red flags.

If both conditions exist, an antagonist is about to attack, and you and others need to respond appropriately. If either condition fails your test, you can probably relax. But take one more look to make sure you didn't miss any red flags.

Early Warning Signs

By alerting yourself to the earliest stages of an antagonist's attack, you gain a distinct advantage. You can minimize the damage done by dealing effectively with the individual before major problems erupt. To this end, consider these early warning signs.

• *A chill in the relationship.* When *a person who is exhibiting red flags* changes his or her manner of relating to you, beware. This might be an initial sign of an antagonistic attack. Where once he or she might have been warm and cordial, now there is icy coldness and perhaps blatant rudeness. When you greet the antagonist in passing, he or she might respond coldly or not at all. He or she might avoid being alone with you—perhaps feeling guilt about his or her intentions, perhaps as a manipulative ploy to upset you, or maybe both.

In group situations, the antagonist might show disrespect toward you, use biting sarcasm (even over trivial matters), or have a condescending attitude. Either way, the antagonist is determined to gain the upper hand and discredit you in front of others.

• *Honeyed "concerns."* As an antagonist begins activity, he or she might pay you a visit or send you a letter of "concern." "I have a concern," can be another way of saying, "I am very angry." Of course, anger can be appropriate and healthy. Both antagonists and nonantagonists get angry, because that is part of being human. *But a red-flag person who expresses "concern" typically means "angry."* Consider the visit or letter as only the first move. More will follow. How *much* more depends on your response to these initial moves.

• *Nettlesome questions.* A red-flag person might begin by asking a number of picky questions, checking out details like: "Where do we buy our mimeo paper?" or "How many times did your board meet last year?" You find yourself feeling nettled as the antagonist becomes a constant fly-in-the-ointment.

• *Mobilizing forces and pot-stirring.* To wage an effective campaign, an antagonist must gather support and create discord, conflict, and doubt. He or she might try any number of approaches to accomplish this end. The behavior could be as innocuous as whispering to others during a meeting. The antagonist might call unofficial meetings, usually not held at the church. He or she might flood the congregation with rumors—not the ordinary kind that plague all congregations, but destructive, insinuating gossip strategically directed against key people. The telephone is a ready tool; the antagonist is "calling just to check some things out," or has some "serious concerns about the congregation or a particular leader" and wants to see if anyone else is worried. As a result, others could indeed become critical, swept along in the antagonist's wake. The force of numbers may give you pause: Could something be wrong with you or your leadership? Ask yourself that question, but don't be overly introspective *if* the source of the confusion is a red-flag person.

• *Meddling.* Another sign of imminent onslaught is a potential antagonist meddling in areas that are not his or her concern. An example would be a red-flag person on a particular committee who abruptly shows an unusual interest in another committee's work. He or she probably has sniffed out a vulnerable weakness. Such meddling is cause for alarm.

• *Resistance.* Finally, you might detect growing resistance and independence from a red-flag person. Resistance might be active, taking the form of openly ridiculing the leadership of the congregation, defying your authority as pastor or lay leader, blocking the approval of certain matters that ordinarily glide through the governing machinery with ease. On the other hand, antagonists might exhibit passive resistance such as withdrawing from an activity while making a public issue of it—emphasizing that his or her nonparticipation is connected with the "concerns" he or she is expressing about the church. Antagonists are typically not content to disappear quietly. Usually they let others know loudly and clearly that they are absent and why they are absent.

The six warning signs presented so far usually come *early*—like the hush before a storm. From a red-flag person, these signs are highly significant. From someone possessing no apparent red flags, the signs might prompt you to reassess the individual in question. The following section describes characteristics of active antagonists at later stages.

Later Warning Signs

Antagonists are not stamped from the same mold; there are probably as many antagonistic behaviors as there are antagonists. Nevertheless, from the diversity of their behaviors certain patterns emerge. A partial list follows, describing typical behaviors of antagonists when their attacks are already well along. Not every antagonist will display all the behaviors; some might evidence three or four of them without displaying any others. In any case, if you encounter an active antagonist, you will witness at least some of these characteristic behaviors:

• *Sloganeering.* Antagonists often use one or more emotionally laden slogans to spread troublesome dissension. For example:

"John is a good man, but not good for this congregation."

"Tom is trying to poison our minds."

"They are communists!"

• *Accusing.* Antagonists frequently bandy about one or more accusations. You might hear:

"You're an adulterer (or racist or homosexual)!"

"You're never (or always) in the office!"

"You're too old (or too young)!"

"You're lazy (or incompetent)!"

And on and on. Accusations such as these often project onto the accused what the accuser consciously or unconsciously feels about him- or herself.

• *Spying.* In more or less obvious ways, an antagonist may begin to spy on you. He or she might telephone to see where you are or even follow you. Antagonists some-times tape-record their phone conversations. A wise rule is: Be as noncommittal as possible when talking on the telephone with an antagonist.

• *Distorting.* Antagonists frequently distort reports of incidents, leaving grains of truth to maintain credibility. For example, if the president of the congregation became slightly vexed during the course of a meeting, an antagonist might say:

"Did you see how the president blew up! Why, such lack of control cast a cloud over the entire meeting! How was a person like that ever elected?"

• *Misquoting Scripture.* Antagonists frequently misquote the Bible to provide proof that their campaigns or behaviors are legitimate. By excising passages from their contexts, imparting their own idiosyncratic meanings to the words, or using various other methods they appeal to a congregation's loyalty to Scripture, falsely equating their causes with the Bible itself.

• *"Judas kissing."* An antagonist is likely to tell the person he or she is attacking, "I am your friend, but this is something that I just have to do." I call this the "Judas Kiss Syndrome," and it can be especially piercing because a church leader may indeed once have considered an antagonist to be a special friend. Friendship thus abused hurts much.

• *Smirking.* A troublemaker might wear an inappropriate smile or a cocky grin when he or she encounters the person under attack. Such a smirk says, "I've got you on the run." It is infuriating, but will gratify the antagonist only if you allow its effect to be perceived.

• *Pestering.* Antagonists sometimes pester church leaders by constantly calling on the phone or by hanging around after a service or a meeting, saying "I'd just like a brief word with you."

• *Letter writing.* Antagonists frequently send letters or other communications. Acknowledge these at first—

perhaps with a *brief* phone call or by sending a postcard with a response such as this:

> Dear _____ :
> Thank you for your concern. I appreciate responsible feedback.
>
> (Signed or initialed)

One of the most counterproductive courses of action would be to respond with a lengthy, single-spaced letter, refuting the antagonist's accusations point by point. A letter of rebuttal does absolutely no good, serving only to add fuel to the antagonist's fire rather than quenching it.

• *Pretense.* Antagonists often portray themselves as champions of the underdog, or as underdogs themselves. The sociological impact of that pretense is usually quite significant. People cheer for the underdog and for those supposedly championing the underdog.

• *Lobbying.* Antagonists frequently lobby with small groups in the congregation to create doubt about one or more leaders. One vulnerable group on whom antagonists focus their attention is new members. This is one reason general education is so important (see Chapter 11).

Sources of Information

Knowledge about the warning signs is helpful, but you may still be wondering how you can gather the information you need in order to tell whether or not an attack is about to begin.

First and foremost, keep your eyes and ears open. Be aware of what is happening around you. If you know the 20 red flags that antagonists wave and can recognize when someone is waving one or more flags, you have a major advantage.

Pay attention as well to the observations of mature, trusted church members. When people you trust and respect make assertions about those whom you might have already recognized as red flag wavers, you would be well-advised to consider what they say.

Listen to what the antagonist says about him- or herself. Oftentimes an antagonist will brag about past exploits—"I sure gave it to the last congregation president who didn't agree with me." Blinded by their own importance and imagining that everyone believes them and supports their cause, antagonists will often blurt out such statements.

You might also want to ask questions. But take care how you do this. You need to be extremely sensitive to the time, place, occasion, and recipient of your questions. A trusted board member who has served faithfully for many years may have observed something. Go ahead and ask, but be discreet and caring.

Finally, trust your sixth sense. Sometimes you sense that something is wrong—a vague uneasiness that a certain individual cannot be trusted. Don't become overly suspicious, but at the same time, grant your sixth sense a fair hearing.

Whatever you do, keep your eyes and ears open. Don't close your eyes and hope that what you don't like will go away. It won't. And if you do nothing, the results could be devastating.

Part Three
PREVENTING ANTAGONISM

How to Maintain an Anti-antagonist Environment

*S*OME congregations seem to have an absence of antagonists, while others apparently attract and activate them. The disproportionate share of attention antagonists demand (and often get) makes it immensely worthwhile for leaders of a congregation to create an environment that is as unfavorable as possible for antagonism. One could put it this way: It's hard to drain a swamp once you are face-to-face with an alligator. "Draining the swamp" and keeping it drained are the subjects of this chapter.

The following fictitious account dramatizes the need for preventive action. The entries are from the diary of a certain Mr. Goodman, vice president of First Church of Anytown, and they accurately depict the impact an antagonist can have both on an individual's life and on the life of a congregation. The story that is conveyed is of the conflicts and difficulties experienced by real people as they live through real encounters with church antagonists.

Sunday, January 6

Already it's the twelfth day of Christmas, but everything in church this morning was as joyous as Christmas day itself. I have good feelings about the coming year, and it will be a pleasure to serve in my new post as vice president of the congregation. We had the pleasure of welcoming a promising new member, Mr. Tagonist, today. Says he wants to be very involved doing the Lord's work in our congregation. When I talked with him after church, he expressed great dissatisfaction with his previous church home, Third Church across town. Seems they didn't appreciate his ideas and efforts. Don't know why. He looks like a likable guy. Maybe the chemistry wasn't right. Anyway, he's sure our congregation is just what he's looking for. And I think so too. . . .

Wednesday, May 8

An unsettling day. Rev. Kindly called me at work and talked about having gone to dinner at the Tagonists. Something is bothering Rev. Kindly, but he doesn't know what. Mr. Tagonist is most charming and full of praise, but—?

Rev. Kindly was surprised to find out that Mr. Tagonist is already the confidant of a number of unnamed people who have concerns. Pastor Kindly asked who they were, but Mr. Tagonist wouldn't say. I listened and hung up feeling bothered, too. I wonder what's up.

Wednesday, March 19 (10 months later)

Mr. Tagonist demanded to be heard at the board meeting tonight, regardless of the fact that he is neither a member of the board nor on the scheduled agenda. The chairperson bent the rules to hear him for 15 minutes, mostly to get him off our backs and quiet him down. Unfortunately, this gesture was unsuccessful on both counts. His arguing and carryings-on continued for over an hour. (I really don't understand why he's so upset.) He took up the rest of our meeting, and we tabled three important items on our agenda, including our final discussion of the list of recommendations regarding our new associate pastor.

Thursday, March 20

I received a telephone message from Mr. Tagonist at work today. I returned the call right away, and he said he urgently needed to explain his position in person to someone on the church board and could we meet tonight. I was busy and, further, I wasn't sure that a meeting of this sort was proper, but I agreed to spend an hour with him. It turned out to be three hours.

Friday, March 21

Today I spent 45 minutes on the phone with Mr. Tagonist during my lunch hour. That man has quite a way with words, but I'm not so sure I can take his side at the board meeting. I asked our minister to meet with me over lunch tomorrow.

Saturday, March 22

Well, Rev. Kindly and I had a good talk today. Rev. Kindly suggested we give an honest "Christian ear" to Mr. Tagonist's objections. We hope our love and openness will bring peace and resolution to his disagreements. The board decided to call an impromptu meeting on Sunday evening and invite him to express his grievances. I hope it works.

Monday, March 24

Last night's meeting didn't satisfy Mr. Tagonist. After listening to him for a solid hour and a half, we still couldn't see his point, and he said he felt horribly misunderstood. I guess we will be taking this matter up again.

Friday, May 16

I have never been to so many meetings in my life—not exactly the most pleasant, either. Have appointment with Dr. Essentialle next week. I think it's my blood pressure.

Thursday, June 19

Bishop Longsuffering visited our congregation again tonight—for the third time this month. He is trying very hard to bring an end to this mess. Although he is definitely a pastor's pastor, I suspect his patience is wearing thin. Good news, though. We finally voted to ask the Rev. Prospect to be our new associate pastor. The board members are excited about Rev. Prospect's upcoming visit.

Sunday, July 6

Rev. Prospect visited our congregation this weekend. A most likable person and very interested in our congregation's ministry. Unfortunately, I saw Mr. Tagonist pull Rev. Prospect aside between services and get a phone number. I heard Mr. Tagonist say, "There are some problems here you'll need to help clean up, Reverend."

Thursday, July 10

Tonight the sad news was reported that the Rev. Prospect respectfully declined the offer to serve at our congregation. I was not at all surprised.

Tuesday, July 22

We had a very depressing meeting tonight. Only 6 of the 15 members attended, so we couldn't move any business. I wonder where everyone was? They couldn't all have been on vacation. We don't have August meetings, so some important business will have to wait until September. But

Mr. Tagonist wasn't absent. He seems to be a regular fixture around here—even more regular and verbal than the official members on the board. I sure hope we don't see him in September, but I imagine that's wishful thinking. This simply must stop.

Sunday, September 28

This is ludicrous. As I sit here at my desk after the annual meeting, I finally see why things are going this way. The problem is not with Mr. Tagonist, but with *us* who have *allowed* him to continue doing these things. But everything seems so out of control now.

Sunday, October 26

I regretfully turned in my resignation from the board today and requested a transfer to Second Church here in Anytown. Pastor Kindly and the others took it quite hard. I felt like a traitor, but I just can't take it any longer.

Saturday, December 20

Mrs. Kindly bumped into Stella and me while Christmas shopping today and apologized for her anger over our leaving. At the time it appeared to her that we were deserting her husband in the middle of the battle, but now they are leaving too. Her husband recently accepted a position as pastor of another church, and they will be moving soon after the holidays. She spoke quite bitterly about the damage to them as a family and to the congregation as a whole. She also mentioned the problems her husband was having as a result of the whole grimy affair: loss of zeal, ambivalence about his sense of calling into the ministry, and sheer exhaustion. He regretted moving, because he felt that Anytown was the ideal place for his ministry, but he knows he has lost much effectiveness. For a while, he toyed with the idea of taking up another occupation. Mrs. Kindly further said that disillusionment is spreading throughout the congregation and worship attendance has dropped off significantly. What a sad, sad mess Mr. Tagonist is leaving in his wake! For the new year, I must resolve never to let a similar situation go unchecked if I ever see one in our new church home.

Mr. Goodman's resolution is a good one for every church leader and member to make. A single antagonist in a congregation can so affect the leaders that they expend what seems to be 90% of their time and energy dealing with one individual. Prevention is the best cure. There are several measures any church can take to create an anti-antagonist environment.

Follow Established Policies

A good way to prevent antagonism is for everyone to follow the established policies and procedures of the congregation. Leaders must never practice or tolerate corner-cutting. Procedures are safeguards against antagonists. Although at times they seem only to tie things up and cause undue headaches, in the end they are valuable aids to ensuring that antagonists will not gain an upper hand in the congregation. If your congregation does not have clear procedural guidelines, consider formulating some.

Functional Feedback Channels

It is always important to establish and use clear channels of communication, but it is essential with regard to antagonism. Two-way, open communication needs to exist between leaders and members. To facilitate this, leaders must clearly tell the congregation what the appropriate channels of communication are, and reiterate them frequently. When clearly spelled out means of response are available, an antagonist who blatantly disregards them is more easily detected and exposed.

Job Descriptions

Clear job descriptions create an unfavorable environment for antagonists. Church board chairpersons, elders, pastors, deacons, and others in positions of authority need to clearly understand their jobs and their relationships with other leaders. Members also need to be apprised of this. For example, if everyone is aware that reactivating inactive members is not the primary job of the evangelism committee, then no one will complain if the evangelism committee failed to visit the inactive Mr. and Mrs. X. Ideally, when everyone understands the delineated lines of responsibility, no one will infringe on another's territory and supply grist for an antagonist's mill. The risks of encouraging unhealthy conflict will then diminish.

Broad Base of Responsibility

A strong, broad base of authority can do much to thwart antagonistic attacks. The authority I speak of here is not the authority over doctrine or souls, but authority in matters of administration and program. When a single individual holds power in a congregation, a one-on-one struggle (usually antagonist versus pastor) often results. When an antagonist realizes that power is carefully distributed among a group of people, then he or she will think twice before instigating trouble.

Discipline That Works

Functional disciplinary measures are also essential to maintaining an anti-antagonist environment. Congregations in which discipline is minimal or absent tend to encourage antagonists. Of course, you will tailor discipline to your own denominational tradition. The crucial factor is this: Whatever your denominational or congregational procedures are in the area of discipline, follow them.

Anticipatory Socialization

Another important technique by which leaders can minimize antagonism is extensive use of "anticipatory socialization." This is psychological shorthand for, "Let people know what you are planning to do before you do it." People tend to resist change, especially in religious matters. If leaders recognize the need for change, they must carefully prepare for it. Change must be gradual and must be accompanied by a great deal of loving commentary. Abrupt change can awaken antagonists.

United Front

Church staff and lay leaders must maintain a united front, with no room for backbiting or unhealthy friction. An antagonist will discover such unhealthy conflict among leaders and use it. A united front does not mean agreement on all things, but mutual respect and support of others in their roles. This frustrates antagonists, who attempt to "divide and conquer."

For Church Staff: A Support Group

A healthy support group for church staff (either one built into the congregation or an ad hoc committee) is extremely helpful in creating a generally uninviting environment for antagonists. This group can work with the church staff to help them to become more competent and effective leaders, offering moral support and constructive criticism to the staff as they carry out official duties. The purpose of the group should not be to supervise the staff, but to give honest, *loving* feedback. A group of this sort keeps the staff in touch with the congregation. It helps minimize unhealthy criticism directed at church staff and further a growth process that is beneficial to all.

Educating the Leaders of the Congregation

*T*HOMAS HENRY HUXLEY once said, "Perhaps the most valuable result of all education is the ability to make yourself do the thing you have to do when it ought to be done, whether you like it or not" (*Technical Education and Other Essays,* 1885). Education indeed equips people to do what must be done, no matter how uncomfortable the task—and few tasks are more uncomfortable than dealing with antagonists. Education about antagonists falls into two categories: *general* and *specific.*

General Education

The goal of general education is to communicate an understanding of the dynamics of antagonism and ways to handle it effectively. Include as many leaders as possible in the process—both church staff and lay leaders. As a minimum, include the chairpersons of all boards and committees. Many congregations already gather these persons together to serve as the primary governing board.

When should general education of leaders begin? Yesterday! It is never too soon. There are distinct advantages to initiating this process apart from an antagonistic crisis. Because you will be able to focus on the topic in a general way, you can treat the subject more dispassionately, reducing the possibility that others will think you are acting defensively.

Who initiates the task of general education? You do, or someone else who cares about the congregation and its ministry. You have already begun this process for yourself by reading this book, and the next step might be to form an educational steering committee. When should this educational process start? Yesterday!

How can this happen? One way would be for a group of individuals to read and study this book, using its companion study guide (*Antagonists in the Church Study Guide* by Kenneth C. Haugk and R. Scott Perry, Minneapolis: Augsburg, 1988). The group might study together over a period of weeks, or focus its learning within the setting of one or two retreats. Along with the benefits for their work in the congregation, leaders and their spouses would benefit by applications of this material to their everyday lives.

What are the purposes of general education? There are two. The first is prevention. Shepherds who recognize the trail of wolves will naturally guide their sheep in a different direction. When church leaders are cognizant of antagonists' ploys, they are better equipped to lead. The second purpose is to provide a foundation for *specific* education when or if it becomes necessary.

Specific Education

Specific education means education about individuals who are beginning to behave antagonistically. Before tackling the subject, you must recognize how sensitive the whole area of specific education is. Handle it with *extreme care*. There are perils here. One danger is that specific education could be the rallying cry to start a witch-hunt. Leaders who recognize beginning antagonism, however, need to share what they see.

Imagine how First Church's situation (described in Chapter 10) might have developed differently if Mr. Goodman or Rev. Kindly had begun specific education of leaders as soon as either of them recognized what was going on.

Specific education should begin where there is a problem and after some leaders have begun to experience discomfort. Ironically, Christians find it extremely difficult to comment realistically about behavior that deserves such comment. Prior general education can help make this necessary process easier. Yet a time might come when you or other leaders will need to nudge people's perceptions and alert them that an antagonist is what you are confronting.

Specific education differs from general education with respect to audience. General education should be available to as many leaders as possible, so they can be aware of the dynamics and treatment of church antagonism. Specific education is for those leaders who bear legitimate responsibility for the problem. If your congregation assigns a separate committee or board to handle disciplinary issues, members of that board, along with those directly involved in the attack, might be the ones who should receive specific education. Another example of a group or particular individuals from a group that might benefit from specific education is a nominating committee seeking qualified candidates for congregational or committee leadership. *It is better to leave a post empty than to fill it with an antagonist.*

Handle specific education tactfully. It might be difficult to say: "Mr. (or Ms.) X is an antagonist," although sometimes the problem is so obvious that these words can be spoken and explained with ease. At other times, specific education should proceed slowly and inductively from effects to causes. Begin to inform selected leaders about ways antagonists usually act. Allow time for members of the group to study the biblical perspective in Chapter 5 of this book. Study the definition and ask the diagnostic questions in Chapter 7, which aid in distinguishing a true antagonist from a concerned activist. Refer to the personality characteristics described in Chapter 7 and the red-flag behaviors described in Chapter 8. If necessary, point out patterns or tendencies evident in the antagonist. Usually the leaders will reason it out for themselves. The more you let the information in this book do the talking, the more likely you are to be taken seriously.

The purpose of specific education is twofold: First, leaders are enabled to assess accurately the particular situation. Second, specific education paves the way for planning strategies to solve the problem, ultimately permitting the appropriate leaders to deal with the situation.

One more word: If you have to do specific education, do so with the greatest love, care, and forgiveness, not only for those in your congregation—the possible victims—but also for the antagonist.

How to Use Authority

*A*UTHORITY in and of itself is a neutral term. The misuse or abuse of authority is bad; the proper, timely use of authority is good and serves as a strong preventive measure against the development of antagonism.

If a physician asked you to diagnose yourself and prescribe drugs for yourself, you would leave his or her office in disgust. Most people have no patience with physicians, judges, government officials, or teachers who refuse to use their proper authority. The same goes for clergy and lay leaders. Those who lead in the church need to learn how to use their proper authority effectively. By so doing, they will do much to prevent antagonism.

If you are a person who has authority, your objectivity may be colored by the basic human need to be liked. This inclination is a positive and healthy instinct that helps people learn to live together harmoniously. Yet sometimes this need goes beyond the drive for healthy social adjustment. The need to be liked can become *the* controlling criterion for every decision and action. All too prevalent in contemporary society, this unhealthy extreme is also present in the church. When a congregation is struggling with antagonism, leaders who overly indulge their need to be liked can bring about damaging repercussions.

Leaders must take a firm (even if unpopular) stand in order to effectively prevent antagonistic situations. Physicians do not usually give prescriptions for their patients based on which medicines taste best, but rather according to what is best for patients' health and well-being. If the medicine tastes bad, so be it. No physician pretends that the side effects of chemotherapy, for example, will be pleasant, and only the alternative makes the treatment endurable. Leadership can be compared to medical treatment. In the absence of crisis, many people would give high marks to likability. But when a crisis occurs, people want leadership, not affability.

People may not like strong leaders, but they hate weak ones. Certainly a potential antagonist will dislike effective actions you take to oppose him or her, and will therefore dislike you. Further, others in the congregation might likewise express discomfort with your firm actions.

Such a reaction is analogous to that of a child whom you roughly push out of the way of a 30-ton cement truck. The child cries because of skinned knees and outraged dignity. Knowing the alternative, you can only hold the child and comfort him or her: you did what was necessary. As in Robert Frost's poem, "The Road Not Taken," each person has a choice to make—deciding which road to follow. For you, the choice is between taking the road less traveled and doing what you know to be right and just, or going down the easier road. Either way, there is a price attached. In order to take the road less traveled (or the narrow road), you may have to lay aside your need to be liked.

What price tags are attached to striving to be liked at the expense of strong leadership in the face of antagonism? Some of them are listed here:

- You lose respect—not only the respect of other leaders and members of the congregation, but your own self-respect as well. You might also cause others to lose respect for the position you hold.

- You come dangerously close to sacrificing your own principles and ethics.
- You lose the trust and confidence of the people you serve, because you appear wishy-washy, always compromising.
- You sacrifice your personal identity by trying to please all the people all the time.
- You force God's mission to take a backseat to your need to be liked.
- You waste time placating and appeasing when you should concentrate your efforts on dealing directly with the antagonist.
- Faced with the impossible (trying to make everyone happy), you may be tempted to resign precipitously when you fail.
- You cultivate a self-centered attitude. Whenever you try to please antagonists and others, you are asking (consciously or unconsciously), "What will they think of *me* if I do such and such?" Striving for the appearance of serving others (and God), you end up serving yourself.
- You cause your family undue suffering.
- You accept the whole problem as *your* particular burden and try to solve it alone.
- You mistake the light of an oncoming train for the light at the end of the tunnel.

You can work so hard getting people to like you that you accomplish the exact opposite, even if you might get some positive, short-term results.

Another human failing is the tendency to blame oneself for circumstances beyond one's own control. We tend to ask, "What did I do wrong?" For example, children often blame themselves if their parents divorce, and adults who should know better reason similarly when confronted by an antagonist. "Somehow, I ought to be able to win this person over, and if I fail, it is my fault."

The antidote for these human failings is proper regard for and use of the authority you possess.

There are two types of authority: *authority of person* and *authority of office.*

Authority of person ultimately stems from your own feelings of worth and ability. The Christian who has grown to possess self-esteem, self-appreciation, and self-celebration is an individual with tremendous personal authority. Think of that older woman in your congregation who is always there when someone needs her. When she speaks, people listen!

Authority of person extends beyond the "heroes of the faith." Even if you might think of yourself as a most ordinary Christian, you are a unique person who possesses an authority quite unlike that of any other.

It makes no difference who you are, clergy or laity; you have authority—unique authority. One of the things that regularly amazes me is how lay members of congregations tend to think that they have no authority. Nothing could be further from the truth. I attended a meeting where a church member requested permission to speak after an antagonist had tormented the chairperson for 15 minutes regarding some trivial issue. The member addressed the antagonist and said, "We've heard you complain about various pastors and other leaders for the last 15 years. Quite frankly, I'm tired of it. Please keep quiet so we can continue the meeting! Thank you."

Her straightforward comment was quite refreshing, and so was the result. The antagonist was so shocked that he didn't say another word all evening, and the meeting ended on schedule. Too often, lay people especially are unaware of the positive power in simply being themselves.

But the authority of person is only half the story. There is also the authority of office. By virtue of an office you hold in the congregation, you may possess additional authority. The limits of your authority will vary from office to office, and from denomination to denomination. Know the extent of your authority with regard to your denomination and your congregation's constitution. In times of relative peace, you might choose not to use some of your authority. In times of active antagonism, however, use your authority to its limit.

Failure to use the authority of your office represents more than just a private decision. In most denominations, because you derive the power of your office from the congregation, your refusal to act is the congregation's refusal. When antagonism interferes with the mission and ministry of the congregation, your anger should embolden you to use every ounce of your authority to end the situation.

To be sure, numerous struggles may go on inside you when you consider dealing with an antagonist. A million intimidating "what-ifs" may crowd your mind: "What if I look like a fool? What if I hurt someone's feelings? What if my own feelings get hurt?" These are proper matters to take to God in prayer. Yet it is a simple fact that to live and act fully entails risk.

At first you might feel terribly awkward using either your personal or official authority. But exercising that authority may also make you feel like a new person.

No one can make you use your authority. It has to be your decision to risk using it. Both kinds of authority have the potential for good. Don't fear them. Use them!

How to Relate to Dormant Antagonists

BASED on what you now know about the characteristic behavior of an antagonist, you should be able to identify such an individual if he or she appears in your congregation. But what do you do then?

Even if a person clearly displays antagonistic characteristics, he or she may not presently be sowing discord in the congregation. It would be inappropriate to treat such a "dormant" antagonist the same way one would an active antagonist. But on the other hand, trying to mollify that person in advance of any crisis would be ineffective.

So what do you do? How should you relate to such an antagonist? The answer is: *very, very carefully.* That is how one should relate to antagonists whether they be active or inactive. You should be no less kind and no less caring in your behavior, but you must be more careful. Your exact strategy and response will vary depending on the level of antagonistic behavior, but in all cases you will need to be on your guard.

There is no one way to properly relate to antagonists. Both you and an antagonist are unique individuals, and therefore your interaction will be unique. Even so, certain actions on your part can reduce the probability of unhealthy conflict, discord, and hurt later on.

Of the principles that follow, some are more appropriate for church staff members; others apply equally to staff and lay leaders.

Act Professionally

First, work at behaving professionally. By *professionally,* I mean be consistent, responsible, and self-controlled. Acting in a professional way in the congregation is not restricted to pastors and other church staff; whatever your position, mature, congruent behavior will serve you well. Professional behavior is a plus for anyone at any time, and is particularly vital when you relate to antagonists.

When you relate to potential antagonists in a professional manner, they might sense a difference without being able to put a finger on it. Occasionally they might ask you (directly or in a roundabout way): "Is something wrong?" At this point your answer should be a simple no. (Nothing *is* wrong—so far.) In the unlikely event that you misjudged them, you will not be forced into backtracking or explaining. Thus your overall demeanor will clear the way for you to relate to them in a clean, uncluttered fashion.

You might think that your reserved behavior will anger antagonists. It might, but there is a greater probability that they will learn to respect you, as a result reducing the chance that they will harass you.

Keep Your Distance

Church leaders are often anxious to open up to others. Anyone who experiences the powerful truth of, "It is in giving that we receive" (Francis of Assisi) is anxious to give to others the precious gift of one's self. But Jesus offered a pertinent warning: "Do not throw your pearls before swine, lest they trample them under foot, and turn to attack you" (Matt. 7:6). When you offer the gift of yourself to antagonists, you are doing exactly what Jesus warned against. Don't run from antagonists, but avoid inviting them to sit at your hearth; the vestibule or foyer is close enough.

Be Accurate

Relating to antagonists requires more accuracy than, "If I remember correctly," or, "I'm almost positive," or "Unless my memory fails me." Don't guess, estimate, or venture any off-the-cuff opinions. An educated guess might be acceptable to most people; to the typical member who asks about average attendance two years earlier, it is perfectly safe to say, "I think church attendance two years ago was just over 250." To a potential antagonist seeking the same information, unless you are 100% certain, say something like, "I'll look it up and let you know." Antagonists are delighted by opportunities to prove others wrong—even slightly—and will seize any chance to catch you in an error.

Be similarly cautious about commenting on spiritual matters. If an antagonist asks you about the interpretation of a Bible passage, offer to look it up, unless you are certain of the correct interpretation. Furthermore, if you know a potential antagonist will attend a given meeting or class, do your homework and be sure of your facts ahead of time. There is an excellent chance the antagonist will try to use what you say against you, so choose your words carefully and prepare thoroughly.

Avoid Excessive Positive Reinforcement

Avoid reinforcing the inappropriate behaviors of antagonists. Even when red-flag persons do something commendable, such as giving a large sum of money or working long hours on a project, don't lavish praise on them.

Excessive praise involves two dangers: First, it raises an antagonist's view of him- or herself. Increasing the confidence of an antagonist feeds the emotional power base from which he or she will launch an attack on you or another leader. Second, by excessively praising antagonists in front of others, you make it easier for them to build a strong following. You will have accorded them special status that they can draw on like a bank balance to cause dissension and destruction later on. A simple thank-you, adequate to the occasion but too small to hoard, can minimize this danger.

Tighten the Reins

When you know an antagonist is gearing up for action, tighten your grip on the reins. As much as you (and other knowledgeable leaders) are able, try to discourage nomination of an antagonist to a position of leadership. You might think that the best place for a red-flag person is as a congregational leader—that he or she will then be too busy to become antagonistic. That couldn't be farther from the truth. The truth is that a leadership role can provide a springboard for the antagonist to create trouble more easily. Encouraging an antagonist to become active in leadership is akin to asking the fox to mind the chickens.

You and other leaders might need to work with your congregation's nominating committee in order to prevent this. Be as honest and direct with the committee as is appropriate—perhaps relating any hard, specific evidence that causes you to question the advisability of placing a particular individual in a leadership position. When you think the congregation would not be best served by a potential antagonist, state this clearly. It is not always possible to prevent the nomination of an antagonist, but do what you can.

Hold Onto Your Gauntlet

In the Middle Ages, knights issued challenges to one another by throwing down their gauntlets. This was their way of saying, "OK, let's have at it!"

In relating to a potential antagonist, do not throw down your gauntlet too soon. I counsel patience. An antagonist's actions must be significant enough to warrant confrontation; otherwise you will appear belligerent. Other leaders might be less aware of the antagonist and his or her potential for destruction than you are. Timing is essential: be sure the time is right.

Hold Your Tongue

In line with the preceding caution about timing, learn to hold your tongue even when an antagonist is provoking you. The point is, don't react—*yet*. The time to deal with the antagonist will come. Responding too soon to antagonists' attacks can be counterproductive. It may mean lowering yourself to their level. It may give them the satisfaction of knowing they have gotten to you with their off-base, off-color, or insulting remarks.

When you respond to the taunts and charges of attackers, they've got you from the start. From an attacker's point of view, the attack is worthwhile only if it causes discomfort for another, and the only way the attacker can know he or she is successful is to see the victim respond in kind—with insults, fists, or tears.

What follows are some suggestions on how to deal with verbal abuse from an antagonist. If you follow them, antagonists' slurs will only bring dishonor to themselves, and you will be better able to deal constructively with your own emotions.

• The truth won't hurt you unless you let it. Sometimes an antagonist makes a statement that is absolutely true. In the course of a meeting, an antagonist might address the chairperson and say, "After all, you weren't even brought up in this denomination. . . ." An excellent response is an unembellished and assertive, "That's right," or total silence. Then move on to the next order of business. To respond by justifying yourself is never wise. Don't waste your time and energy; a response elevates the accusation to a significance beyond what it deserves.

• Don't seek sympathy from others. It might work at first, but this strategy won't benefit you in the long run. Eventually you will wear out your welcome. Even your friends and supporters could start to see you as a whiner— precisely the opposite of the impression you want to impart. In a potentially antagonistic situation, the operating rule is: Weakness invites and prolongs attack; strength repels it.

• Don't request a special committee to handle the accusations of the antagonist. Some people think along these lines: "We'll get a committee of three upright folks to sit down and listen to the antagonist's grievances, and perhaps reach a peaceful resolution." This is unproductive. The action only increases the apparent credibility of the antagonist's accusations. Forming a committee will magnify the very problem which you want to nip in the bud. Committees tend to drag on and on, wasting everyone's time except the antagonist's, who relishes the attention. The members of the committee will grow sick and tired of the whole affair. (At this point, I am describing only a *defensive* committee. I am *not* saying that a committee or board should never deal with an antagonist. Part Four will point out that there are times when positive action by a committee—one prepared to deal with the antagonist—is in order. But not at this time when the goal is to stop the problem cold.)

• Don't call for a vote of confidence. If someone suggests one, don't encourage it. A vote of confidence forces everyone to take sides when you and other leaders want to play down the importance of the antagonist's attack.

Your attitude should be one of blithe self-confidence, presuming that you have the support of others—and helping to ensure that you *do* have support. Avoid opinion surveys for the same reason. Show your self-respect by avoiding the masochistic display of obtaining public performance ratings.

Defend yourself against a potential antagonist's behavior by brushing it off as a petty annoyance—or better, no annoyance at all. Your attitude must communicate a sense of imperviousness to attack, as should that of the boards and committees of the congregation. Response encourages antagonists, so follow the advice of Proverbs 26:4: "Answer not a fool according to his folly, lest you be like him yourself."

Don't Recommend Counseling

Antagonists have problems, to be sure, and you might consider them candidates for counseling. Out of concern for their personal well-being and your desire to prevent full-blown antagonism, you might decide to recommend professional counseling or psychotherapy for the individual.

Although recommending counseling sounds worthwhile on the surface, it is inadvisable. First, because of their personality makeup, antagonists very rarely follow through on the referral. If they view everyone else as wrong and themselves as right, why should they seek help? Second, your recommendation of professional help is likely to place antagonists on the defensive—backing them into a corner—almost guaranteeing that they will lash out at you.

Many of the relational guidelines in this chapter may appear to be the exact opposite of how you think you should normally behave. If you are a pastor, many of them fly in the face of what you expect of yourself as a church professional. Emotionally you might have difficulty implementing these suggestions, although rationally you might see their validity.

Your choice boils down to this: You can operate from strength early on, dealing with antagonists calmly and nondefensively, or you can react later, when the situation mushrooms out of control, threatening to damage you and the whole congregation. An ounce of prevention now is worth more than a pound of confrontation later.

The Value
of a Confessor-Confidant

AS YOU collide with an antagonist and struggle with a pile of problems collapsing on you, you can receive invaluable assistance from a confessor-confidant. You can likewise be of invaluable assistance to another who might be taking the brunt of such an attack.

A confessor-confidant is someone with whom you can share feelings, thoughts, and strategies for coping with an antagonistic situation. You can risk trusting a confessor-confidant, revealing to him or her your true feelings. He or she will respect confidences, display a measure of objectivity, listen intently, and offer responsible, timely advice.

Note that "become your friend" is not among the functions listed above. The person you seek out need not be your friend, nor should you necessarily expect the relationship to develop into friendship if you are filling the role of confessor-confidant for another. Friendship may happen, but that is not essential for the relationship to be helpful.

If You Need a Confessor-Confidant

Many people think that needing a confessor-confidant shows weakness or inadequacy. In truth, it is a sign of health to recognize that individuals need one another. Strength lies in interdependence. People who believe that strength means going it alone scarcely fool themselves—and certainly not others. Healthy people realize that God did not make us to be strictly independent.

If you think a confessor-confidant would be beneficial, where do you look for one? If you are a lay person, perhaps the most obvious candidate is your pastor, although other lay leaders can serve as good confessor-confidants too. If you are a pastor, you need help and ministry from confessor-confidants every bit as much as lay leaders—if not more. A responsible lay person who has demonstrated an ability to keep confidences might be someone with whom to develop a confessor-confidant relationship. You might also cultivate this kind of relationship with another staff person. Perhaps the church staff could work together as a group in this regard.

I usually advise pastors, in particular, to find a confessor-confidant *outside the congregation.* This person will need to be someone who has sufficient time for you, as well as concern for your situation. He or she must be accepting, empathic, and (more important yet) someone who will maintain confidentiality—maybe a neighbor or a friend. A pastor might consider a neighboring colleague. Occasionally a judicatory official might be a possibility, but not always. You need more time than most judicatory officials (who are responsible for many clergy and congregations, not to mention administrative details) can give. A judicatory official, however, might be able to help you find a confessor-confidant.

How do you establish a confessor-confidant relationship? To be sure, you are asking a lot of someone, probably a significant number of hours before you are through. The best way is simply to approach another, explain your situation, express your need, and ask if he or she is willing to help you:

> I have some things I need to talk about. We have a serious conflict going on, and I am at my wits' end. I sure could use a listening ear and maybe some advice. I was wondering if you could give me some time?

Of course, the other person might say, "No, I don't think I can help." If so, don't take it personally. You will undoubtedly find a suitable confessor-confidant sooner or later. In such a situation, where a conflict is already raging, you might ask the person who agrees to serve as your confessor-confidant to read this book as the first order of business.

If You Are Needed as a Confessor-Confidant for Another

You might feel hesitant to venture out as a confessor-confidant for another. Don't be afraid; you might be the very person to help. But there is only one way to know for certain: Take the risk, offer your time, interest, and care to that other person.

As confessor-confidant, you are free to *initiate* care, unlike a professional psychotherapist, for example. If you have recently attended a meeting in which an antagonist viciously attacked an individual, leaving that person obviously distressed, go to him or her. Say that you observed the antagonist's behavior and offer yourself as a listener. Perhaps the person will decline, but often this response stems from a desire not to impose. When you know the other individual clearly needs help, be assertive and let that person know how important it is that they find a confessor-confidant, even if they may not be comfortable with you in that role.

After your offer is accepted or someone approaches you requesting your help, you may want to formalize the relationship by establishing a regular meeting time and place—for example, once a week at a certain time for an hour or so. This is particularly necessary if the individual is experiencing a severe crisis. In so doing, you become accountable for helping the other person, who will now be able to depend on consistent help. You might say, "I will make this time together a high priority; you need to do the same. This matter is too important to treat lightly." In a very real sense you will function as a kind of counselor to that person. Essential to that relationship is commitment. Discussing confidentiality is also vital in formalizing the relationship. At least once, and probably more often, explicitly state that what you both talk about in your meetings is totally confidential. The other individual should never fear that you will divulge to others what he or she says to you.

During the meetings, focus on the *other person's* needs. Your purpose is not to pass the time in idle chatter. Keep the meetings focused on the problems and the emotions of the other person.

Be conscious of how much you talk. If the other person talks 75% of the time, well and good. Certainly you can easily express relevant ideas and strategies in 25% of the time. When a more directive approach is called for, then, of course, speak as much as necessary, but continually monitor how much you are talking.

Also beware lest you cross the hazy border between *empathy* and *overidentification.* While you may suffer with another, you suffer as *yourself,* not the other person. If you enmesh yourself in the other's problems, you become unable to relate objectively to his or her needs, taking those needs upon yourself. Then you will be far less effective.

A good confessor-confidant relationship will include a certain amount of education. Don't allow education to intrude into emotional cleansing, but inevitably a time will come when the other person asks, "What did I do wrong? What can I do differently? Can you help me?" At that time you stand on the threshold of a teachable moment, and you help clarify for the individual what an antagonist is and is not. Inform him or her that antagonists are a disturbed minority. Discuss the red flags that identify antagonists. Help the person to look at past interactions—what he or she did right and wrong—and consider future strategies. You might role-play upcoming situations together. Suggest helpful reading material you have discovered.

A confessor-confidant affirms the other as much as possible. You will be dealing with individuals who may be experiencing significant hurt and whose confidence in their leadership ability has received a terrific jolt. You have the privilege of helping them revive their damaged sense of self-worth and leadership capacity. While you will aim much affirmation at the person's leadership, affirmation from the heart builds and strengthens the other's whole person, renovating what the antagonist has tried to tear down.

Although your focus will probably be on a single individual when you function as a confessor-confidant, be alert for possible stress in the family as well. If you determine that the family needs caring too, suggest that the other family members consider establishing a similar relationship. If it is within your capability, you and your family might be of assistance in caring for that family.

Distinctively Christian spirituality should fill the confessor-confidant relationship. Jesus meant his promise, "Where two or three are gathered in my name, there am I in the midst of them" (Matt. 18:20). Take God seriously. The time you spend ought to be enfolded in the clasp of a prayerful relationship. God is present. God is able to fortify and sustain both of you. In general your times together will not be prayer meetings (though at times this might be appropriate), but don't neglect the powerful resources God has placed at your disposal. Pray when you deem the other person needs it, and continue to remind him or her of God's continuing presence and love.

As confessor-confidant you have a further responsibility: to be available at times outside your scheduled meetings. Tell the other person that you are available whenever he or she needs you. Telephone care and consultation can be valuable for the other person as he or she makes various decisions and plans tactics. Communicating availability also infuses the relationship with the in-depth care that transforms lives: "You matter to me, and I will do all I can to help you through this."

Recognize your own limitations and plan accordingly. There may be situations beyond your ability to help—for example, dealing with someone who is severely depressed or suicidal. When necessary, arrange for that individual to see a professional. When in doubt, you might consult with a therapist to learn whether referral might be in order. On occasion, you and the therapist might work together in a cooperative arrangement.

Beware of overextending yourself. For example, it is probably unwise to act as confessor-confidant to more than one or two people at a time. Helping more individuals than that is likely to induce you to "cut corners" with them, and this is neither healthy nor fair. Serving as a confessor-confidant involves a significant amount of time if done correctly. Make sure you give the other person as much quality time as he or she needs.

In summary, do what you can. When you choose to be a confessor-confidant, you have the tremendous privilege of helping someone regain his or her sense of self-worth. You can do so because you have the knowledge, you are willing to listen more than you talk, and you bring your reliance on God into the fray. The trust required of you, whether you need a confessor-confidant or could become one, is immense. Is it simple? No. Is it Possible? Absolutely!

Part Four

DEALING WITH ANTAGONISM

Invisible Antagonists

*S*OMETHING is happening. A subtle disturbance within the congregation is causing ripples on the surface. The precise source and location of the problem are obscure, but something is stirring. You notice a few signs that little by little add up to trouble. It's as if you were sitting in the woods and suddenly noticed that there were no birds singing and no animal noises to be heard. What now? What can you do?

The situation places you at a disadvantage. You are visible; the antagonist is invisible. Despite the disadvantages, however, you have a number of options. Here are some positive actions you can take:

1. Be the best possible leader you can be, and continue to do your job effectively. Do everything in your power to continue the mission and ministry of the congregation or group you are serving.

2. Don't panic or bring other activities to a screeching halt while you wait for the antagonist to reveal him- or herself. Don't go on a fact-finding mission or expend large amounts of energy searching out the trouble and its source.

3. Accept the fact that it is not critical to precisely identify the antagonist or antagonists. Ask yourself, "How important is it that they be brought to the surface?" Strive for an attitude that says, "This matter is not sufficiently important that I need allow it to interfere with God's mission for this committee or congregation and the work entrusted to me and other leaders." Seeking the antagonists out could cause more trouble than ignoring them would. (Most certainly, if serious damage occurs and people and ministry are being hurt, the antagonist must be identified and confronted. But if significant damage is being done, you will undoubtedly know who it is anyway.)

4. Act confidently. Remember the operating rule when dealing with antagonists: weakness invites and prolongs attack; strength repels it. An air of confidence is one's best defense.

5. Note the locations of tension and disturbance. If the meetings of a particular board were full of tension in September, October, December, and February, and charitably productive in November and January, check the attendance records. You might find that person X was absent in November and January. Don't exaggerate the importance of the correlation, but pay closer attention to person X. You *might* have stumbled onto something.

6. A final recourse when you don't know the source of tension is to live with it. People will always be critical, and you will never be in a situation where somebody isn't griping about something. Acknowledge the reality of imperfection in all of life, including congregational life. The "conflict-free church" is a myth, and recognizing this can help you adapt to this reality.

There is another way in which early tremors can present you with a problem. You yourself may be fully aware that a particular individual is an antagonist, but unfortunately:

• no one else may see the signs and symptoms; or
• the antagonist may be a church leader; or

- others may pretend not to notice (denying the facts); or
- no one else may be willing (thus far) to act.

What can you do when an antagonist is just beginning to make the transition from invisibility to visibility?

For starters, not much—at least not right away. There are two reasons: First, if you lack the support of others, you handicap yourself considerably in dealing effectively with an antagonist. One pastor, who was in a situation where an antagonist was evident to him but to no one else, put it this way: "I could see the self-serving nature of the antagonist very early on, but no one else did. I was left alone, holding this idea while my wife and others consistently criticized me for *not caring*." Second, sitting back and waiting is sometimes all you can do, and may even be the best possible action. Be patient. As the book of Proverbs points out:

A fool flaunts his folly (13:16).

A fool throws off restraint and is careless (14:16).

A fool's mouth is his ruin (18:7).

By being patient you merely allow antagonists to publicly reveal themselves.

Invisible antagonists—unseen either by you or by others—present you with an opportunity and a challenge. The opportunity is to get on with the work of the church. The challenge is that you need to maintain vigilance and be ready to respond when the antagonist begins to come forward.

How to Conduct One-to-One Interviews with Antagonists

*T*ENSION. It fills the room, pressing in on you and making it hard for you to breathe. You want to focus on the individual seated across from you, but when your eyes meet, you are the first to look away. You can feel the other person looking at you with a pitiless, hostile stare, icy and implacable.

Your mind flits uncertainly from one question to the next: "What do I say? What can I do? Will I need to meet with this person again? How should I act? Will reason work? Maybe if I could show that I care." Round and round you go.

The other person, who has come expressing "concerns" about you and your leadership, seems oblivious to the tension, a study in composure and self-confidence. It is only too clear who wrote the script, assigned you the tragic part, and now directs the production: *the antagonist seated across from you.*

Does a meeting with an antagonist have to be like this?

Absolutely not!

As you study the recommendations that follow, remember that they are based on the assumption that there is no doubt that you are confronting a true antagonist. You *know* it. And because you know it, you also know that this person is hostile.

Your certainty of the other's unrelenting hostility is what will give you the conviction to act in the strong ways you will find recommended here. If someone threatened violence to a child, to a friend, or to a defenseless animal, how would you respond? The same surge of feelings and sense of responsibility you would experience in those situations would be justified—and also helpful—when you are facing an antagonist.

Responding forcefully but responsibly to someone who is waving numerous red flags of antagonism is what this chapter is all about. The following quote from William Manchester clarifies the need for assertiveness. In his account of the first of five attempts by the U. S. Senate to censure Joseph McCarthy (this one under the leadership of Maryland Senator Millard E. Tydings), Manchester wrote:

> Tydings' confidence was ebbing. He was being outfoxed and outbludgeoned, and he was too skillful a politician not to sense it. While he was shaping the report—which would be read only by Americans already aware of McCarthy's infamy—public support for McCarthy continued to grow.... Tydings had won all the battles of reason and decency, but McCarthy had never tried to be reasonable. (William Manchester, *The Glory and the Dream,* Boston: Little, Brown and Company, 1973, pp. 647-648.)

The principles presented in this chapter are firm, and necessarily so. The characteristics of antagonists demand firm, assertive behavior when you interact with them. To act otherwise is to court failure.

The opening scene of this chapter is a disaster in the making, which you can prevent by paying heed to three critical aspects of an interview with an antagonist:

- Setting up the meeting
- The arrival of the antagonist
- The interview itself

In the material that follows I will assume that you are dealing with someone who is severely antagonistic. You will need to temper the approach if the individual with whom you are dealing is less severely antagonistic.

Who should guide the interaction? is the key question in dealing with antagonists, because control of you and the situation is what the antagonist is after. If the antagonist is able to gain that control, the potential harm to you and to your group or congregation is incalculable.

The primary focus in this chapter is not on how to handle antagonists, but how to handle *yourself.* The ability to take charge of yourself is essential in one-to-one interviews with antagonists. By controlling yourself and certain environmental factors, you seek to ensure that the destination you reach is yours, not the antagonist's.

Bear in mind that these suggestions are meant *only for use with antagonists.* You would act very differently when you deal with most people, and rightly so. The point is that antagonists are not "most people," and thus warrant a much firmer approach.

Setting Up the Meeting

Setting up the meeting begins at the point an antagonist contacts you and ends when he or she arrives to talk. These activities may appear to be insignificant, but they are crucial for setting a tone for everything that follows.

- *Who contacts whom?* If possible, avoid meeting with the antagonist at all. *If there is to be a meeting, it should be at the antagonist's initiative.* Of all the variables discussed in this chapter, this one is the most important.

Requesting a meeting with an antagonist is asking for trouble, trouble that the antagonist would be only too happy to provide. When *you* make the initial contact, you communicate to the antagonist that you are the one needing to get together and talk. You place the antagonist in control of that aspect of the situation.

You might be tempted to think that initiating a meeting will be the best way to clear up misunderstandings. *Resist that temptation.* Meeting with an antagonist might temporarily quiet him or her, but not for long. You will end up sacrificing self-respect, self-control, and control of the situation. If antagonists entice you to come to them, you demonstrate weakness and vulnerability—and they will capitalize on it. You may even end up pleading with them to stop. In most cases, antagonists do not respond positively to attempts at reconciliation.

The only exception to the "principle of noninitiation" of meetings is when a board or committee takes firm action (discussed in Chapter 19). Only in that case should you—together with other leaders—initiate a meeting with an antagonist.

• *Where do you meet?* The location of a meeting with an antagonist is another critical factor. When they initiate meetings, antagonists sometimes suggest that you meet at their office or home. Meeting with them on their turf only gives them added confidence.

A special problem arises if you are a pastor who typically visits people in their homes, and an antagonist asks you to visit him or her there. What do you do? Avoid this by suggesting an alternative:

> How about if you stopped by my office? I think that would be preferable. We will be better able to talk there.

Be firm in your intention to meet *in a place of your choosing.* If you do not have an office or similar convenient place at which to meet, you may even want to use someone else's. If you are a lay leader, you might suggest getting together in a church office or meeting room. A neutral location is preferable to a place of the antagonist's choosing.

Avoid holding the meeting in your home, however. Allowing an antagonist into your home can create unnecessary complications. All of us have learned a whole set of "host" behaviors, and we tend to fall into them automatically. You might have trouble changing some of them in order to behave in the assertive way necessary to deal with antagonists. Embarrassing personal or family situations could also occur, giving the antagonist additional data with which to criticize you.

Reality makes nonsense of packaged answers, of course, which is why I am giving you principles rather than absolutes. Some pastors, for example, have their offices in their homes, so meeting there may be unavoidable. Adjust these suggestions as your circumstances require, but stick to the principle: *You* choose the meeting place.

• *"How about lunch?"* Antagonists will occasionally invite you to have lunch with them in order to discuss their grievances. I advise not doing so. A meal creates an unwanted atmosphere of intimacy that will work against you. Besides, you may be the intended main course!

If you meet with an antagonist for lunch, you face a number of problems. There may be interruptions, and you will not be free to take many of the steps discussed in this chapter to maintain control of yourself and of the situation. Certain actions demonstrating firmness can be done in an office, but would be inappropriate in public. There is also the question of who pays for lunch. The antagonist will probably want to pick up the tab—thereby asserting a measure of control over you.

If an antagonistic individual says that he or she wants to meet about serious concerns and suggests a lunch engagement, calmly say something like, "I think it would be better if we met in my office." If the antagonist persists, continue to assert your own wishes. Don't allow yourself to be taken to lunch. The time for you to establish control is when you set up the meeting, not at a busy eating establishment.

• *"Can I come over right now?"* Sometimes an antagonist will call with an air of urgency and ask (or demand) to meet with you right away. What do you do? First of all, ask the antagonist what he or she needs to talk to you about. The person might be involved in a personal or family crisis and genuinely in need of help. If so, by all means meet with the antagonist as you would with any other person who needs care. If the individual tells you that the crisis concerns your leadership or related subjects, however, that is different. Here, permitting the antagonist to intrude on your schedule amounts to handing over control of the situation. Don't do it. If the antagonist refuses to tell you what he or she wants to discuss, it probably is not a personal crisis needing immediate attention. You might want to say something like:

> This is not a good time right now. What about getting together tomorrow morning at 11:00 for an hour?

You need not be more specific than that. Your schedule is your own business. Should the antagonist demand to know specifically why you can't meet, you can simply say, "It's not possible right now."

• *When do you meet?* Along with not meeting immediately at an antagonist's request, it is inadvisable to meet at any other specific time the antagonist suggests, even when this might be possible for you. It is, again, a matter of taking charge of the situation; you determine the time. If an antagonist suggests that you meet at 9:00 A.M. the next day, you may want to say something like:

> Nine is not a good time for me. How about 11:00? We can sit down for an hour at that time.

Notice that such an approach permits you to set the beginning time of the meeting as well as to set limits on the overall length of time you plan to meet. Antagonists tend to think they have the right to take liberties with your schedule. By specifically mentioning that you plan to meet for an hour, you are establishing a structure for the meeting from the start. Most of the time they will not take issue with that statement when you first make it. If they demand more time, you might respond by saying:

> I think we ought to be able to deal with everything in an hour if we are efficient about it.

Don't be forced into setting up an open-ended meeting or setting aside more time than you wish to give. If you do, they will have taken control of the situation. Furthermore, they will be able to acquire more ammunition for their campaign of insinuations and gossip if you then cut off the meeting when they "still had so many important things to say."

The dogged persistence of antagonists tends to wear people down. Meeting with an antagonist at length weakens your resistance, aiding and abetting the antagonist's cause.

If possible, schedule your meeting with an antagonist before another commitment—for example, an 11:00 A.M. meeting with an antagonist when you already have a luncheon scheduled at 12:30. If you arrange your schedule this way, be sure to end your meeting promptly when the hour is up. Don't fall into the trap of extending the meeting. This not only is disrespectful to your 12:30 commitment, but it also gives the antagonist a degree of power over you. Cutting off antagonists at the scheduled ending time demonstrates your authority. Even though it may temporarily upset them, in the long run it will prove beneficial.

• *What about witnesses?* One possibility that might seem attractive to you on first thought is to have a witness present during the interview. This would be a mistake. It escalates the situation far more than you want to, and consequently inflates the antagonist's ego. The antagonist may also ask to bring someone, which you should firmly reject. Say something like, "We can accomplish what we need to without another person present." If the antagonist brings someone anyway, or brings someone unannounced, politely have the other person wait while just you and the antagonist meet. Make no apologies. Simply state: "This is a private meeting with X at his (or her) request."

The only exception to the principle of meeting without witnesses is when the appropriate church body or board has decided to take disciplinary action (as described in Chapter 19).

The Arrival of the Antagonist

The suggestions that follow cover the period of time between the antagonist's arrival prior to the meeting and before the substantive portion of the meeting begins. What happens during this arrival period is likewise crucial.

• *When do you begin?* Whether you begin early, on time, or somewhat late can subtly influence the tone of the meeting and determine who will be in charge of the situation. It is inadvisable to begin early, because this conveys to the antagonist your willingness to be accommodating, which the antagonist will be quick to interpret as a sign of weakness. The fact that you see yourself as a representative of reasonableness and decency must not blind you to the nature of the person you are dealing with: antagonists are on the prowl for signs of weakness, which they will then attempt to exploit.

Some antagonists make a practice of arriving early for interviews. Not anticipating this can catch you off guard and put you at a distinct disadvantage.

If you are a pastor and have a secretary, advise the secretary ahead of time to invite the antagonist to have a seat. If you don't have a secretary, anticipate the antagonist's possible early arrival by having your door shut. If the antagonist arrives early and knocks on your door, open it slightly and say, "I'll be out in a few minutes." In some situations, you might not have a private office, making it easy for an antagonist to walk right in. In this case, you could decide not to arrive at the designated location until the agreed-upon time for the meeting.

Along with sometimes coming early to catch people off guard, antagonists occasionally arrive late to try to establish control in their favor. If the antagonist is late, engage in some other task in the interim, such as returning a telephone call, and complete it even after the individual arrives. Thus, you express to the antagonist that your time is valuable and will not be wasted. If the antagonist then asks about your tardiness, tell him or her that you were ready at the appointed time, but when he or she was not there, you returned a telephone call. That's the truth and the truth is difficult to dispute. Finally, if your meeting with the antagonist was originally scheduled to conclude at noon, stick to that original agreement.

• *How do you greet them?* Perhaps you typically greet people with a friendly smile and a cheery hello, paving the way for them to share their needs and concerns with you. With antagonists, however, your greeting might well be different. Ask yourself if you are in fact genuinely happy to see them. Respond to antagonists in a way that is more congruent with how you feel. A simple hello spoken in a business-like tone would suffice. An ambiguous greeting, disclosing little about your feelings, prevents an antagonist from being deluded into thinking that he or she has control of you and of the conversation.

• *What about seating?* Who sits first? This might seem unimportant, but how you work out seating is very significant. As you and the antagonist enter your office, simply resume your seat. It might be wise to forgo inviting him or her to sit down. Eventually, the antagonist will sit, but for a brief moment will be uncertain whether he or she belongs there or not.

The height of your respective chairs is also important. Sitting higher than another can give a slight but definite subliminal advantage in the situation. Make sure the antagonist's chair is not higher than yours.

If your desk faces into the room, have the antagonist sit across the desk from you. Talking across a desk provides emotional distance and a feeling of protection.

• *What about coffee?* Should you offer coffee or not? Here's another item that might seem of minimal importance. It actually is important because offering a beverage can be a relational act, part of making a person feel at home. But the intimacy associated with offering food and drink is counterproductive when you relate to an antagonist. Forgo this gesture of hospitality, unless doing this would be very awkward and unusual for you.

How to Conduct the Interview Itself

The following suggestions cover the heart of the interview itself—what happens from the time the antagonist is first seated through the end of the interaction.

• *Who should talk first?* The preliminaries are over. The antagonist is seated, and the interaction is about to begin. Who should start the conversation? When dealing with antagonists, do not do what you would normally do. Resist the temptation to "bridge the gap," to get the conversation going. Let the antagonist speak first. Don't worry. He or she will have plenty to say, and there is no need to make it easy. Look silently at him or her. Don't look expectantly or give any nonverbal cues. Why build a bridge over which the antagonist can walk to give you trouble?

• *How much should you talk?* Many people talk too much when meeting with antagonists—perhaps from defensiveness, habit, or the false assumption that reason and logic will help the antagonist see things correctly. With antagonists, however, your best course of action is to keep relatively silent. The more antagonists are able to engage you in conversation, the better off they are. Saying little and maintaining a solid presence (steady eyes, good posture, minimal fidgeting) is far more beneficial than words.

• *How should you listen?* Be an attentive listener, but not an active listener. Active listening involves using verbal and nonverbal cues to encourage conversation. With an antagonist, you want to do the opposite. Any reinforcement, positive or negative, leads the antagonist to continue talking. Joel Greenspoon's research on operant conditioning supports this principle. Greenspoon set up fictitious interviews, instructing the interviewers to say, "Mmmmm-hmmm," each time the interviewee used a plural noun. He found that the subjects unconsciously began to use more and more plural responses as a result of this subtle conditioning (Joel Greenspoon, "The Reinforcing Effect of Two Spoken Sounds on the Frequency of Two Responses," *American Journal of Psychology,* vol. 68 [1955]: 409-416). Your use of verbal and nonverbal encouragement can similarly reinforce an antagonist's aggressive behavior.

• *How "noteworthy" is the interview?* Take notes at every meeting with an antagonist. Why? First, your notes will serve as a permanent record of the meeting—for future reference. Second, taking notes indicates that you are gathering facts. Taking notes also relieves you from having to maintain constant eye contact. (Some eye contact is important; it communicates strength to the antagonist.)

What if an antagonist asks to see your notes? Simply say "No," which is your perfect right. If an antagonist presses further and asks why not, very matter-of-factly say, "They are mine." If the antagonist demands to see your notes, use the broken record technique and continue to say "They are mine," or "No." After the interview your notes should be kept in a place where no one else has access to them.

• *What about tape recordings?* Do not tape-record an interview with an antagonist. It would be incendiary as well as nonproductive. Telling the antagonist you intend to record the interview further escalates the importance of the encounter, which you want to avoid at all cost. (Incidentally, secret taping is unethical.)

Tapes are useless in any event. You could never use them as a defense—the inferences of "police state tactics" and subterfuge are too sinister. Other church leaders would rapidly tire of listening to recorded conversations and would almost certainly look askance at *you* for making the tapes in the first place.

If the antagonist requests to tape the meeting, firmly decline. If the antagonist presumes to tell you he or she intends to tape your meeting, insist that you "do not conduct for an unseen audience" meetings intended for the mutual benefit of two people. If the antagonist persists, just end the meeting.

• *How do you handle questions?* Antagonists frequently ask questions to try to trick you into saying something that they can use against you. Many such questions are obviously hostile, and you will know exactly why he or she is asking them. Apparently harmless questions can also cause problems. For example, if you are a new staff person, an antagonist may ask, "How do you like it here at Calvary?" Avoid answering in detail, which will give the antagonist less opportunity to misconstrue what you say or repeat your answer out of context. A good response to this sort of question is: "Fine." If the antagonist persists in trying to drag an opinion from you, continue to say, "Fine," or "Great," or whatever.

Antagonists may ask your opinion of certain church policies. Certainly you would feel free to discuss such things with responsible people. If an antagonist does this, however, one way to respond is, "Well, that's the church's policy." The antagonist might say, "But what do *you* think about it?" Your response could be, "I'm comfortable working within the church's policy on this matter. I am sure the policy was established thoughtfully."

Sometimes an antagonist might ask you about something he or she would like to see done (or undone). For example, if your church is doing something different in Sunday morning worship, and you are the head of the worship committee, an antagonist might say: "Do you intend to change back to the old way of doing things?" Answer this type of question simply by saying something like, "This is the way the committee has decided to do it." If the antagonist directly asks if something might change, say, "That is something for the committee to discuss." He or she might persist, saying something like, "I know full well that you have the power to make those decisions yourself." Neither deny nor confirm the antagonist's statement. Continue by saying, "This is something the committee needs to talk about."

Sometimes an antagonist will ask questions to which either a positive or negative answer will give you trouble. For example: "Don't you think the squabbling between the mission board and social ministry board is shameful?" One way to answer is to say, "I hear you." The antagonist won't want to accept such an answer, and he or she might persist. Remember the broken record technique. Remember, too, that you have no obligation to answer unfair or irrelevant questions. It is your right to answer or not answer a question as you please. If you remind yourself what antagonists can do with such information, you will probably agree that discretion is the better part of valor.

• *Should you challenge them?* Be firm with antagonists, but avoid challenging or arguing with them. Challenging or arguing with antagonists produces no good, and there is very little possibility that you can change their minds. You also run the risk of further agitating them, fueling the campaign after the interview.

Take care also not to bait antagonists. Resist any temptation to make fun of them, even if they make ludicrous statements that tempt you to laugh as you simultaneously feel your anger rise. Your natural desire might be to respond sarcastically, but that only angers them more. Refrain from putting them down. You may need to bite your tongue, but a sore tongue is better than added fuel for an antagonist's fire.

If an antagonist tries to argue with you by falsely accusing you of something, answer firmly but don't deny the same thing over and over. Deny the charge once or twice, and then say, "You heard what I said."

• *What about physical danger?* You *might* be in physical danger as you meet with antagonists. This occurs in a minority of instances, but it is still important enough to note.

If you think a person is potentially dangerous, you might refuse to meet with him or her. You need to draw the line, even if this means sacrificing part of your reputation as a thoughtful, caring individual. If you do decide to meet with a potentially violent person, take some precautions. Perhaps you could meet with the door open and have another person close at hand, either in the next office or otherwise nearby. Clear your office ahead of time of articles that potentially could be thrown: heavy ashtrays, scissors, and so on.

Sometimes the potential for violence telegraphs itself via rising decibels or nonverbal clues after the interview has begun. Whatever you do, don't touch the person. Terminate the interview as quickly and gently as possible.

Handling interviews with antagonists can be summarized by four points:

• **Work.** You must be willing to work hard to conduct the interview.
• **Risk.** You will be called on to act in ways that might not appear to be effective in the short run, but will prove

themselves in the long run. Trust the process and courageously try out new behaviors. They work.

- **Belief.** Believe that what you are doing is right and act in accordance with that belief.
- **Genuineness.** The core of your response will come not from learning new techniques, but from recognizing and accepting your genuine feelings. In this way you will be able to act in a congruent, firm, and healthy fashion.

Confidentiality
and Documentation

*C*ONFIDENTIALITY and documentation are two key issues that have ethical overtones. Both require your thoughtful consideration of the principles involved. Trust among church members and between church members and clergy is a fragile thing, dependent on the assurance that confidentiality will be respected. Documenting a person's history and behavior can threaten that trust, and therefore the issues involved need to be examined with much care.

Confidentiality

To tell or not to tell, that is the question. And if to tell, then whom to tell and what to tell? With a decided lack of Christian charity, an antagonist may have been attacking you or someone you care about. You feel variously hurt, threatened, angry, and intimidated. The antagonist has been insulting, gossiping, disruptive, and harassing. You bottle up quantities of information and emotion inside, and you ask yourself, "How much of this is confidential?"

Almost every church leader struggling with an antagonist asks this question. There are generally accepted guidelines that will help you decide what is a breach of confidence and what is permissible to discuss.

Confidentiality always applies in counseling-related situations. If an antagonist has been in a helping relationship with you in the past, you must keep that information to yourself—even if it could help explain the antagonist's present behavior to others. When you are entrusted with confidential information, you must not break that trust.

Confidentiality applies less strictly in situations other than specific helping or counseling relationships. For example, you are certainly free to discuss "public knowledge," that is, behaviors that others can easily observe. Many interactions that do not take place in a counseling-related context are not confidential, and may be shared discreetly with responsible people at appropriate times—while never permitting this freedom to decay into a pretext for gossip.

Since antagonists usually wage campaigns that are public, the matter of confidentiality is nearly always irrelevant. If an antagonist publicly slanders your person, office, or performance, this is hardly confidential. Actually, most antagonists are delighted when you discuss their allegations with others, because they think discussion will aid their cause. If you have the slightest doubt whether a communication from an antagonist is confidential, ask the antagonist for permission to share what he or she has just said. The antagonist most likely will be happy to grant you permission. You might also want to inform an antagonist ahead of time that all conversations with you are exempted from confidentiality. Hallway encounters within the earshot of others do not fall in the category of confidentiality.

Matters that you would ordinarily decline to mention—in a spirit of long-suffering—in times of antagonistic attack should be shared with the proper boards or leaders. With discretion, and guided by the preceding statements about confidentiality, you are certainly able to disclose information to the appropriate leaders so they can proceed effectively with their jobs.

Does confidentiality apply to antagonistic situations? When an antagonist is waging a public campaign, the answer is basically no. The preceding suggestions do not cover every conceivable situation, but keep them in mind. If a particular circumstance is unclear, exercise your common sense and let your best judgment, care, and concern for the church and its mission be your guide.

Documentation

The decision to document the behavior of individuals with marked antagonistic tendencies is also one with ethical implications. Decisions you reach may come to you only after painfully struggling with this question at length. If, after weighing ethical considerations, you choose not to document, that's all right. But there are certain situations in which the existence of documentation will serve you and others well.

The procedure is fairly simple. If you discover that person X manifests numerous behaviors that are clearly antagonistic (for example, if X displays a convincing combination of red flags), you might begin to document that person's actions, not only for your own protection, but also to protect the congregation.

Documentation can include several different kinds of information. First, you may want to keep a rather extensive private record of anything written about you, especially articles, announcements, or other items that might be construed as somewhat controversial. This file may include community newspaper clippings, religious publications, memos, and minutes of relevant meetings. Sometimes antagonists will flash old material in your face and accuse you of misconduct. If you keep a thorough file on yourself, you will never be trapped in the discomfiting position of failing to remember what was written about you.

Second, file away any and all written communications that you receive from antagonists, and keep copies of the responses you make. Antagonists frequently lie. When you can show your past communications with an antagonist, his or her lying does little harm. For example, if person X insists that you never responded to his or her overtures to discuss certain disagreements—but you actually did— you will have the substantiating information available.

Third, you may also want to make note of any verbal communications the antagonist makes to you. Here you should strive to be extremely objective. For instance, do not write, "Person X is getting rather obnoxious, continuing to call about those silly demands." Instead, write, "Person X called today (include the date), at 6:30 P.M. for the fifth consecutive night to express displeasure with my nonaction regarding X's opinions offered at the council meeting on February 23. X said I was incompetent, unchristian, didn't care about the congregation, was motivated by the Devil, and that X would do everything possible to get me off the board." Such a behavioral emphasis lets the *actions* of X do the work without your own editorial intrusion into the narrative.

Documentation ensures that the details of what X did or did not do, and what you did or did not do, will be beyond reasonable dispute. When other church leaders are reluctant to face up to the seriousness of an antagonistic problem, you can let the data do the talking, and the facts can move them to appropriate action.

You must also reckon with the reality that some antagonistic encounters, albeit rare, will end in a court of law. Whether or not you would intend for the matter to go that far, the antagonist himself (or herself) might press it to that unpleasant point. Your defense in such situations could well depend on your thorough and complete records.

Take the same precautions about security of these documents as you would any other papers dealing with highly confidential matters. If you should leave your position in the congregation, take them with you or (preferably) destroy them.

Public Communications Regarding Antagonism

WHEN antagonists are active, church leaders frequently experience anxiety over what to do. Sometimes they are tempted to resolve their anxiety by turning to the various public communication channels readily available to them. Several appealing, but illusory, possibilities may suggest themselves: to try to settle the conflict; to inform the congregation about the problems an antagonist is causing; or to communicate with the antagonist and hope he or she will hear and change (or perhaps to express feelings simmering inside). Here are some examples of such unfruitful attempts:

From a Sunday morning sermon:

> God commands all those who are his children in Christ to preserve the unity of the Spirit. There is not, indeed there cannot be, room for gossip, lying, backbiting and slander among us. When we fall into these behaviors, we only demonstrate to God, the world, and to each other how very far we are from his will.

From a prayer offered by the vice president of a congregation at the annual meeting:

> Finally, Lord, we ask that you provide a large measure of healing to this congregation. Forgive us for quarreling. Help us to be open and up-front with each other, always putting the best construction on everything.

From a letter to the congregation by the chairperson of the governing council:

> It has come to our attention that there are those in this congregation who disagree with certain policies set forth by the duly elected council. If anyone is dissatisfied, he or she should speak with us first. There are appropriate channels for expressing disagreement, and spreading untruths and dissension are not among them.

Communications of this sort hold a certain appeal. On the surface, they seem to confront the problem directly. They appear to be an open, honest expression of true feelings. But there is one serious drawback to this approach: most of the time it fails miserably. There are a number of reasons for this.

• *Using channels of public communication to combat antagonism gives the antagonist attention and recognition, reinforcing the negative behavior.* Despite your intentions, the antagonist may relish the publicity. He or she might be overjoyed at your acknowledgment. You might feed a martyr complex, which thrives on what the antagonist perceives to be verbal or written persecution. On the other hand, the individual might feel threatened, pushed into a corner, and increasingly angry. By arousing his or her ire, you throw coals on the antagonist's fire. Either way you lose.

• *Using channels of public communication to combat antagonism could be perceived as taking unfair advantage of your position.* Even those who agree with your assessment of a given antagonist might frown on your use of public communications to deal with the matter. It might appear that you are playing unfairly, despite the fact that the antagonist has probably been unfair to you or others. For example, preaching sermons "at them" leaves antagonists no direct recourse. After all, they could hardly stand up after you finish and say, "I would like to have my say now."

• *Using channels of public communication to combat antagonism can create doubt where there was none before.* Shakespeare expressed it this way: "The lady doth protest too much, methinks." When people defend themselves in public, the public begins to wonder about them. Wise parents know better than to warn their children against doing things their children would never think to do on their own. "Don't put beans in your nose" is a foolish thing to say. The individual who stands before a group and says, "I have been accused, though not to my face, of _____ . I want you all to know that it is not true," plants public doubt where none may have existed previously. So does the church leader who announces, "There are those who would like to see me gone." Many accusations are best not brought to public attention.

• *Using public communication channels to fight antagonism creates an unhealthy atmosphere for the whole congregation.* In effect, you drag the entire congregation through the gutter. Many members might be blissfully unaware that anything is wrong. Once you go public, however, you make everyone aware of the unfortunate situation. You create pain and anxiety for many who are helpless to do anything about the situation anyway.

• *By alluding to antagonism through public communication channels, you can appear to be weak.* If you reveal deep and intensely personal feelings on the matter, you can expect disrespect and ridicule from some. At least in the present age, many people are unprepared to deal with that level of openness. There is also the question as to whether it is appropriate. There are proper times and places to share feelings, and there are times and places not to share them. Such sharing can be frightening, and those whom you lead might misunderstand. By doing this, you can devalue yourself in others' eyes—appearing unable to control yourself, let alone able to function effectively as a leader.

• *Using public communication channels to fight antagonism could make you come across as an ogre.* Publicly venting your indignation is as ineffective as venting your fears. In this case, you serve only to make people afraid of you. Granted, no one will think you are a weak leader, but demonstrating that kind of strength is undesirable. "Getting tough" in a newsletter, from the pulpit, or elsewhere is only self-defeating. You do not want to scare your supporters away.

• *Using public communication channels to address antagonism violates the use for which these channels were intended.* Prayer is for speaking to God—lifting concerns, needs, and thanksgiving—not for taking an oblique jab at antagonists. The pulpit is the place to proclaim God's Word, not the place to vent emotions or hurl venomous arrows at an antagonist. Newsletters are for communicating information, for networking, and for offering encouragement. Using channels of public communication for anything except their intended purpose is to abuse them.

Leadership Issues

*T*HE leaders of a congregation will take the brunt of an active antagonist's attacks. Although everyone in a congregation has the theoretical responsibility for dealing with an antagonist, it is the leaders who for the most part will be confronted with the hard, practical necessities. Therefore leaders must prepare themselves both tactically and strategically for dealing with antagonists in group situations, for presenting a united front, and for the difficult decisions associated with disciplinary measures.

How to Handle Group Situations with Antagonists

Any meeting with an active antagonist present has the potential to degenerate into a three-ring circus, featuring the antagonist as ringmaster. Consciously or unconsciously, antagonists carry two questions into group situations: How can I get control? How can I disrupt? Whether a group will dissolve into chaos or maintain orderly flow and continue to accomplish the business at hand depends on how you and the rest of the group respond.

• *Chairpersons.* If you preside over a meeting in which an antagonist creates trouble, you are in a strong position to deal with the situation. A confident, direct, and bold chairperson is often able to handle an antagonist virtually alone.

To do so most effectively, it is imperative that you thoroughly understand the level of authority that is vested in you. This may involve reviewing portions of the congregation's constitution and by-laws, and perhaps dusting off a copy of *Robert's Rules of Order.* In any case, do your homework. Know how far you can legitimately go in setting and enforcing an agenda at a given meeting, and use all your legitimate authority to hold the meeting to that agenda. Know when an item of business or procedure is out of order, and do not hesitate to say so. Many rules and policies were established for just such occasions.

When you are willing to assert your authority and studiously follow orderly procedures, you gain the control that enables you to steer the meeting away from the dangerous shoals of antagonism into a peaceful harbor where meaningful work can proceed with minimal disruption.

• *Members.* If you are a board or committee member, you also have an important part to play in keeping antagonistic friction to a minimum. Don't think for a moment that you are powerless; quite the contrary! The average committee member sometimes can stand up for common sense and fairness with greater effectiveness than the chairperson. Imagine the effect on a meeting that has been derailed from its purpose by an antagonist if a member asks for the floor, stands up, and says, "Let's get down to business. My patience is wearing thin, and I am wondering if I speak for others too. Thank you." Words like these will often silence antagonists.

The average member also has a *vote*—a most potent weapon against the arrogance of antagonism. Formally moving to close discussion with a second from the floor can have a powerful and beneficial result. An informed, courageous, and conscientious committee member can make a significant impact on controlling antagonism in group situations.

• *Ex-officio members.* Many congregations have ex-officio members sitting on boards and committees. In a number of congregations, the pastor is an ex-officio member of all boards. In some congregations the president is similarly privileged. This ex-officio status may be short on official privileges, but it is long on influence.

A well-chosen word delivered from a respected advisor can go far to preserve good order. For example, I once sat in on a meeting of a congregation's governing board where an antagonist rambled on nonstop. The chairperson was evidently too embarrassed to stop him. Finally the pastor, present as an ex-officio member, raised his hand, was recognized, and asked for the floor. The chair granted his request. The pastor rose to his feet and said, "I think the Word of God has something to say here," and then, in a powerful voice, read Romans 16:17-18:

> I appeal to you, brethren, to take note of those who create dissensions and difficulties, in opposition to the doctrine which you have been taught; avoid them. For such persons do not serve our Lord Christ, but their own appetites, and by fair and flattering words they deceive the hearts of the simple-minded.

When he finished, he looked around, decisively shut his Bible, and took his seat without another word. Heavy silence followed. The chairperson pulled out a handkerchief, wiped his brow, and said, "I guess we can proceed to the next order of business." The antagonist did not say another word the entire evening.

In whatever capacity you serve as a member of a committee or board, you can be the one who either locks the door on chaos or throws open the doors and bids it come in. Don't hesitate to fulfill your position to the utmost. Remember Edmond Burke's warning that all it takes for the forces of disruption to triumph is for good people to do nothing.

The Phalanx: A Unified Front

The word *phalanx* is the technical term for a military tactic developed by the ancient Greeks. A well-armed infantry unit stood together (shoulder-to-shoulder, shield-to-shield) about eight men deep, thus forming a mobile, almost impenetrable wall of defense.

There is a lesson in this for congregations that face the attacks of antagonists. Congregational leaders would do well to form a phalanx, especially when dealing with the more tenacious antagonists. The shields are not composed of bronze and leather, but of the *spirit of working together,* united against the invader. When presenting this united front, realize that the success of your phalanx depends on the degree to which leaders function as a consistent, unified whole. The weakness of one individual's stance can prove disastrous.

Adopt the phalanx tactic when all roads to reconciliation have failed and the possibility of a creative, healthy resolution is remote at best, *but before serious damage is done by antagonism.*

Paul gave Titus this mandate: "As for a man who is factious, after admonishing him once or twice, have nothing more to do with him" (Titus 3:10). The phalanx technique is an effective way to comply with the apostle's advice. Its purpose is to preserve the vitality of members and ministry by eliminating the dissension introduced by an antagonist.

"Divide and conquer" is the principle by which an antagonist seeks to render church leaders ineffective. If the antagonist can incite leaders to disagree or fight among themselves, many of his or her goals are met. As

Jesus observed, "And if a house is divided against itself, that house will not be able to stand" (Mark 3:25).

Church leaders might take a cue from one principle of effective parenting. When a child manipulates or misbehaves, parents may disagree on the limits to be set or on appropriate punishment. But if they're smart, they won't disagree in front of the child—or even worse, behave inconsistently.

The way children sometimes try to play off the "softy" against the "toughy" bears a striking resemblance to the way antagonists try to pit church leaders against one another. Church leaders differ in strength when it comes to standing up to antagonists; some are softer, some tougher, just as parents are. Keeping each other informed is the church leaders' key to prevention of this "divide and conquer" ploy, just as it is for parents.

Good communication among leaders will serve as your best shield against an antagonist's attempts to divide. Establish a system in which others are promptly notified if the antagonist contacts (or pesters, as the case may be) one leader. Relay rapidly whatever information you gain in the encounter. This kind of communication serves two functions. First, the person contacted receives support of others in resisting the temptations to succumb to the antagonist and his or her demands (thus weakening the phalanx). Second, should the antagonist approach another leader, that person will already be aware of the probable line of attack and will be adequately prepared to ward it off. Such a hot-line not only maintains, but also strengthens, your unified front.

The ultimate goal of the phalanx technique is *extinction* of the negative and divisive behaviors manifested by antagonists in the congregation. Extinction is the process by which certain behaviors are eliminated through nonreinforcement. With antagonists, this involves refraining from favoring them with further attention, which only serves to reinforce their destructive behavior.

Extinction is relatively difficult to accomplish. Psychological experiments have shown that even the slightest reinforcement will keep an established behavior pattern alive. Much effort toward nonreinforcement can be sabotaged by a single leader deciding to operate independently, thinking it won't hurt to lend a sympathetic ear to the antagonist "just once." In truth, it will hurt, because any kind of reinforcement will induce the antagonist to continue or escalate his or her destructive behavior. Implementing a phalanx means that each leader agrees there is no such thing as operating independently when confronted by an antagonist.

Disciplinary Measures

By the time matters have reached the stage where a phalanx is called for, it may be that disciplinary measures appropriate to your own ecclesiastical tradition are also called for. Christian denominations vary in their respective approaches to church discipline. Yet despite the variety of practices, some basic understandings exist across denominational lines.

Chief among these common themes is the principle that one who offends must be corrected for his or her own good and for the good of the congregation. Yet in spite of this principle there is often a deep reluctance on the part of pastors, lay leaders, and entire congregations to apply Christian discipline. The result is that while disciplinary procedures exist "on the books," congregations often make every effort to avoid putting them into practice. In many situations of life, a caution like this is undoubtedly healthy. The admonition of Christ still rings in our ears: "Let him who is without sin among you be the first to throw a stone . . ." (John 8:7). In the case of antagonists, this reluctance is extremely unfortunate and inappropriate. Once you have determined that you are dealing with an antagonist, you no longer need to be so cautious; indeed, *you must not be.*

When specific disciplinary actions are called for, the leader's responsibility is not to equivocate or bend the regulations, but to carry them out. In this area there is no room for improvisation.

Act scrupulously according to the procedures your congregation or denomination has spelled out. Sometimes the circumstances in your church may escalate to the point where you need to call in outside help (this is discussed in the next chapter).

Sometimes church leaders worry: "What if we discipline a member, and others leave?" While the fear may be real, it should not be a factor in the decision. If discipline is called for, it must be carried out. Otherwise the church forfeits the right to be considered an advocate of truth and justice.

The (Mostly) False Hope for Change

There is another way in which rationalization interferes with exercise of leadership, and it has to do with entertaining the wishful hope for a turnaround on the part of the antagonist. It is a mostly false hope. *Mostly* false. Can an antagonist change? Certainly. Change *can* happen, even when it seems impossible. But the issue is not possibility—it is likelihood and actuality.

False hope is aroused when people refuse to face the likely and probable, clinging only to the possible. I'm not minimizing the possible, but stressing that your hope might be mostly false if you cling only to the possible. Anyone might change, because God is a living, active God. Yet as long as you think *only* in terms of the possible, you speculate with little basis in reality. There comes a time to move beyond dreaming about a rose garden to facing squarely the dandelion-and-crabgrass reality that exists. The fact is that antagonists tend *not* to change.

Some leaders are too proud to admit that they cannot turn an antagonist around. It is frustrating to realize that one can do little or nothing to help antagonists grow toward wholeness, especially when "helping" is part of one's job description. Wedded to that frustrated pride is some guilt. "What did I do wrong? What can I do now to repair it?" If you are troubled by such feelings of guilt, talk it out with your confessor-confidant or someone else you trust. Your sense of guilt is probably unfounded, but you feel it nonetheless.

How can you avoid being trapped by the false hope for change? By accepting reality. If you question an antagonist's resistance to change or wonder whether a certain troublesome individual is indeed an antagonist, refer again to Chapters 7-9. Realize that the hardened will of the antagonist can perhaps only be changed by God. God entrusts you with plenty of responsibilities, including praying for the antagonist—but remember that you are also called to help care for and protect the body of Christ of which you are a part.

You Are Forgiven

Another problem experienced by church leaders is the perfectionism trap. This trap is so subtle and inviting that many church leaders unknowingly stumble into it and never discover the way out.

Perfectionism begins innocently enough: the whisper of a suggestion to yourself that maybe, just maybe, you should be a little better than you are. You begin to take on more and more, telling yourself all the while that you can handle it. Then you start thinking that you must never make mistakes.

Some perfectionists refuse to recognize their human fallibility, clamping more rigid controls on themselves and setting more unattainable standards. Some eventually throw in the towel, saying in effect, "If I can't be perfect, then I won't play." Some continue the pretense that perfect behavior is possible, because they are unaware of an alternative. And some perfectionists painfully and slowly learn, "I'm not perfect, and that's all right."

Antagonists look for weaknesses to exploit, and they are only too delighted to confirm a perfectionist's tendency to blame him- or herself. An antagonist will nail the suspicion of a mistake firmly to a perfectionist's hide, and gladly go forth to broadcast the news. Because perfectionists are only too willing to blame themselves for flaws, they cringe before abuse from an antagonist.

Only God has the right to be a perfectionist. The idea that you can achieve God-like perfection in your life does not come from God; it comes from the other camp and is meant to drive you to despair. The forgiveness of God is marked "For Sinners Only." That's the good news that keeps me going every day. I say to myself, "I am a sinner; I am imperfect; I make mistakes. I do some things right; I do some things wrong. Therefore, I am one whom Christ can save." What better news could there be for any church leader, for any human being? Once you experience that forgiveness, the "I have-paid-it-all-for-you-ness" of Christ on the cross, you can be freed from the paralysis of perfectionism.

Both clergy and lay church leaders spend entirely too much time castigating themselves when attacked by antagonists, as they transform fear of being judgmental into ruthlessness toward self. Since God finds you innocent in Christ, it is rather unwise for you to continue telling God that he is wrong.

You're not perfect, and that's all right. If you were, you would not need Jesus Christ. You need to surrender the antagonist to God's care. And you need to surrender yourself to those same loving arms.

Personal and Family Variables

*T*O SOME extent, you are in control of how much an antagonist affects your personal life and relationships. And it is important that you exercise the control that you do have.

The four stories that follow reflect the typical effects of antagonism on families in a congregation. Although the individuals named are fictitious and the stories reflect an imaginary situation, the effects of antagonism that arc portrayed and the emotions involved are true to life.

Reverend Johnson's Story

I remember how everyone was so anxious before the meeting. Should the congregation stay where it is and refocus its ministry to the much changed (and seemingly ever changing) neighborhood around us, or accept Mrs. Smith's gracious offer and relocate in the suburb where she was willing to donate the land?

The congregation studied intensively the choices confronting us. There were pluses and minuses on both sides. There were valid points to staying in the city. Valid points to moving our location. The needs of both the present and future members were taken into consideration. Where did mission and ministry call us? Many of us were really torn until all the clarifying facts were in.

After months of discussion and prayer, the congregation voted overwhelmingly to stay and address the needs of those in the central city, so Mrs. Smith's offer was graciously declined. Now that the matter was settled, a sense of peace spread over the congregation. I thought!

Mrs. Smith was somewhat miffed when the congregation turned down her offer, but she smiled and said she had no intention of leaving her congregation—even if she thought they were making a big mistake. A few families left after it was clear that the congregation was not relocating, but all in all, the matter seemed to die an easy (and relatively painless) death.

How naive I was! About six months after the decisive meeting, my son told me he had overheard his Sunday school teacher telling her husband that Mrs. Smith was deeply concerned about my leadership skills and neglect of the older members. She thought I was spending entirely too much time with the new folks.

I dismissed this as the usual gossip that can grow in congregations. About a month later, however, my wife was more or less hostilely confronted by Mrs. Smith. "Have we older and faithful members of this congregation insulted your husband in any way, Mrs. Johnson, to account for the way he treats us?" My wife was taken aback. She stammered out a quick and incredulous, "Why, no, Mrs. Smith, of course not. I don't know what you mean." My wife came home in tears.

Before I could contact Mrs. Smith to discuss the matter, the phone rang. It was the president of the council, who was calling an emergency meeting next Sunday evening to discuss, as he put it, "... growing dissent in the congregation."

I was astounded. Too much was happening too fast. What could I do? When I reached Mrs. Smith, she curtly replied that she would speak with me at the council meeting and not before. I became increasingly irritable, and I wondered how God could permit such injustice.

I still made my regular visits that week, and most people were wonderfully receptive, especially Gertrude W_____. She was always a joy to visit. But a few people who were formerly very cordial and polite seemed distant. Maybe it was my imagination. Eventually I discovered that Mrs. Smith had been calling people to tell them what was "really" happening in the congregation. In the days before the meeting, I was so preoccupied with the problem that there didn't seem to be enough hours in the day. I slept poorly and so did my wife, because I continually rehashed events with her. Headaches and heartburn were the norm. If anything went wrong at home, I reacted out of all proportion.

At the council meeting on Sunday, Mrs. Smith dominated the meeting with accusations that I discriminated against the long-time members of the congregation. I came home flabbergasted. My wife listened to the report and confessed that she was feeling real hatred for Mrs. Smith and the rest of the congregation. The whole affair was absolutely miserable, and the worst part, she said, was that I had become so entangled in my problems that I had forgotten about my family. For the first time in 17 years, our anniversary came and went without my noticing it. I tried to apologize to my wife, but she didn't seem to understand. I also learned that my son had been in some trouble at school, but I was so busy trying to dispel Mrs. Smith's accusations that I was unavailable to help. Most unbelievable of all, my wife had told me about it five days earlier, and I had nodded my head without hearing a word.

Gertrude's Story

My congregation means so much to me. Ever since Harold died six years ago, they have become my family. My children all live far away and lead their own lives. Reverend Johnson is such a friend. When Harold first got sick, he came to see him at least once a week. After Harold died, Reverend Johnson was always available, as were several other members of the congregation. Such dear, dear people. Now I can't bear to see what's happening. I just can't believe what that Mrs. Smith says about him. At first I wasn't thrilled about worshiping next to her, but Reverend Johnson and the others helped me to see that we are all one in Christ. I realized how wrong I was and moved beyond it. I just don't see why that Mrs. Smith is reacting like this, and I don't understand why they pay so much attention to her. It really hurts to see our congregation tear at one another like this. At my age, I don't want to fight constantly. It makes me tired. I excused myself from the women's meeting last week, because I didn't want to listen to the bickering and insinuations there. I've seen enough fights in my day. Maybe if I were younger, I wouldn't be so upset . . . I don't know, I just don't know.

Brent's Story

I've seen it before, but now it's happening in our church, and people hesitate to do anything about it. Ten years ago, the place where I worked needed to refurbish the old plant or move to the new industrial park. One of the vice presidents was all set on the move, and he was furious when we decided to stay. (I think he lives out in that direction.) He said we were real fools. Actually, it was far more cost-effective to stay in our present location. Well, anyway, this man started sowing discord. Eventually, after much tribulation, he was fired. The whole experience was unpleasant. Although my company let that go on too long, at least we did something about it.

Reverend Johnson cares too much about what Mrs. Smith thinks, and so do most of our other leaders. They are constantly thinking of new ways to appease her.

I got into a tangle with her about eight months ago because I was on the committee researching possibilities for renting additional space in the neighborhood. I remember her at the fact-finding meeting when I announced that we could obtain the storefront property for peanuts. How she glared! When she tried to give me a hard time about starting those programs, I ignored her. I knew where she was coming from. I guess she finally gave up. I've got better things to do than waste my time with her.

And now this. I'm fed up with the whole thing. I've given my best to this church, and now they're going to let a sore loser tear it all to pieces. At our last board meeting, all we did was talk about how to handle this whole mess. I was all set to report on that gymnasium we could use on Friday evenings, but that was tabled. Hey, if this is ministry, I want no part of it.

I used to reserve Sunday mornings for golf. My wife, Sandy, is the one who convinced me to get involved in church. At first I went just to please the family; then I came to enjoy it myself. Reverend Johnson is tremendous. When my folks were killed in an accident two years ago, he was something else. I really respect him even if he is a bit too accommodating for my tastes.

There's no way I'm going to stand around and watch all this crumble. If I want to fight, I can do that outside the church.

The kids are upset. Why shouldn't they be, seeing their dad walking out on the church? They're too young to understand. My wife is taking it all quietly, but I can tell she's upset. What can I say to her? I've seen this happen before. I know where it's headed if they don't stop that woman, but no one is tough enough to do it.

Sandy's Story

My husband Brent talks tough, but he's really not so tough. He's rather soft inside. In fact, I've heard him talk like that before. It's usually when he's hurt—and scared.

I remember five years ago when Brent wasn't active in our congregation. He said he didn't believe in God, and he was a different person in other ways too. I mean, he was knotted up inside, preoccupied with business. Don't get me wrong—he's always been a good husband and a great businessman. It was just that sometimes he seemed to treat me and the kids like business partners, not like a family.

Things are so different now. He's still a top-notch businessman, but he's a changed person since—well, since Jesus found him at our church. Some say it was the church—you know, the social thing—and Brent even talks like that sometimes. But it was deeper. I know Jesus Christ is transforming his life. I really fear what will happen to him if he cuts himself off from spiritual nourishment.

I worry constantly that we will slip back into the kind of life we were leading five years ago. Now Brent is preoccupied and short-tempered. He comes home steaming mad from church meetings. I've tried to caution him about the effect on the children when they hear him ranting about the church, and then he bites my head off.

The other day I suggested we try another congregation. Brent said "No way! I know the world is full of people like Mrs. Smith, and I'm not about to watch that kind of tragedy again." If only he could see the tragedy that he's playing into right now.

Throughout these four stories are hints of the ways antagonists affect family relationships. Irritability, preoccupation, physical disorders, guilt, anger—all these and more can spill over to those you love. When church staff are involved, the issues can be as basic as eating: "Will I continue to receive a paycheck?" Anxiety compounds the other problems.

Although the catalog of ways family relationships can suffer is long, there is a more important question to address: What can you do to interrupt the cycle?

Protecting Your Family

Prevention is of course the best antidote. If you head off antagonism before it becomes active in your church, you do more to protect your family relationships than any after-the-fact "cures" will accomplish. You can overcome the effects of poison, but how much better never to have ingested it in the first place.

Even with the best of intentions, prevention is not always possible. When you find yourself caught up in an antagonistic situation, here are some ways to protect your family from the stresses induced by antagonists:

• Cultivate a solid devotional and prayer life for yourself. Seek God's will in prayer, including personal quiet time in which you listen as well as pray.

• Guard your family from the effects of displacement. An antagonist will arouse anger, fear, anxiety, and many other feelings, with the strong likelihood that they will spill over to those you love. In part, you can control how much of this emotion you communicate to your family. You can also warn your family that you are having a bad time, and that what might appear to be bad feelings toward them will in truth be the result of pressures on you.

• Talk with your spouse and children (to a reasonable and proper extent) about what is happening. "Reasonable and proper" depends on your judgment. You need the support of your family, and your family needs the opportunity for growth through supporting you. At the same time, you know the strength of your family unit, and it is certainly possible to overwhelm your family. Talking with a confessor-confidant, as described in Chapter 14, gives you an opportunity to defuse some of your more explosive emotions without involving your family. Your goal is to aim for optimal, not maximal sharing with your family.

• Be aware of your feelings and keep lines of communication within your family open. Everyone should feel free to discuss feelings about the antagonist. Information from this book might also be helpful to family members who may not fully understand the dynamics of the situation.

• Share positive aspects of your church life as well as negative ones. If your children hear only negative reports from you, they might be turned off by church, and turned off to Christianity.

• Schedule a devotional or quiet time with your family as well as yourself. Pray together or share in some activity that emphasizes God's power for healing and promise of justice. Reading the Psalms can provide a good focus for a family devotion. Many writers of the Psalms certainly knew how to express anger.

• Schedule recreational time with your family and be firm about honoring the commitment. Look for activities that demand your total attention, so that you are unable to discuss the antagonist. Roller coaster riding might be just the thing. Hiking or some other form of exercise will help to ease your emotional overload.

• Schedule time for yourself. Relax by doing what you like to do—exercise, hobbies, reading, listening to music, and so on.

You may not be able to do all these things, but do what you can; any such action will have positive results. In the midst of your personal dealings with an antagonist and the accompanying furor, you should strive to minimize the damage an antagonist causes.

Denominational Support Structures

*O*RGANIZATIONALLY, there is great diversity across Christian denominations. In some denominations, congregational autonomy is the rule; in others, an extended hierarchy exists. Specific procedures for proper referral of matters of concern may exist at either of these two poles, while between them are all the gradations of support structures you might expect. Despite this diversity, there are a number of principles for congregations to follow that apply to almost all situations where at least minimal support structures exist.

First, before any problem arises, you should search out and learn your denomination's own way of handling matters such as antagonism. Common sense, not to mention sound ministry practice, dictates such a "stitch in time." Some denominations already have in place effective ways to handle antagonistic conflicts. Members of a denomination might be quite unaware of the regulations and procedures simply because they have never had a need to apply them. Learn those rules and procedures and follow them in your own congregation as fully as possible when an antagonistic situation develops.

Second, as a rule of thumb, always try to handle the problem at the congregational level. This is not to say you should avoid seeking the counsel and support of denominational officials, but do recognize that the less *openly* involved a judicatory official is, the better. In general, it must not appear that the official is "interfering" in the congregation's business. Open intervention by a church official is usually a last resort after local efforts to resolve the crisis have proved unavailing.

When you do turn to your church officials, you can expect a range of possible responses, from care and concern to advice and mediation to—unfortunately—neglect and avoidance of the issue. You may reasonably require interpretation of your denomination's by-laws and procedures, for example, and denominational officials can serve as valuable resource people for this purpose. In some instances they may fill a mentoring role, or be able to suggest a confessor-confidant.

The third principle is this: *Notify early, but request help late.* One frequent complaint of denominational officials is that too often they are the last to know there is trouble in a congregation. Judicatory officials should always be kept appropriately informed of potentially explosive situations, for a number of reasons:

• They can be much more effective if not caught unaware.
• At an early point an official might be able to provide some crucial advice, insights, or assistance.
• The official might be in a position to arrange for a consultant or staff person who has specific skills in shepherding congregations through such times of antagonistic crisis.

Judicatory officials want to know when a storm is beginning to brew, not when all they can do is help a congregation clean up the wreckage. Notifying them at an early stage helps keep better control of the situation. Antagonists may make threats such as, "I'm going to call the bishop." You can experience peace of mind knowing the appropriate authority already knows about the situation. In reply to such a statement you could unperturbedly say, "The bishop is already aware of this situation." Offer no further explanation.

In general, the pastor is the one to initiate contact with judicatory officials. He or she might find it advisable to invite informed members of the lay leadership to join in any representations that are made. A lay leader who has witnessed or personally experienced a particular antagonist's attack is likely to have specific information to aid judicatory officials in assessing the magnitude of the problem.

Fourth, in communicating with judicatory officials, be specific. Report facts. Avoid evaluative statements or generalizations about the antagonist. Concentrate on describing behaviors. The following example clarifies the distinction between evaluative and descriptive reporting.

Evaluative	Descriptive
John was extremely disruptive, combative, and threatening at the church council meeting last night!	At the meeting of the church council, John stood up and started talking without being recognized by the chair and then accused the president of "devising the budget for the furtherance of the kingdom of Satan." When asked what his specific objections were to the budget, John kept repeating rather loudly, "I know what you are up to.

You can't fool me." After asking John to calm down a number of times, the president politely asked him to leave. As he was leaving, John said, "I'm going to get you. Just wait until the congregation hears about this!"

Evaluative reports are too limited. In the evaluative report here, the church official merely found out that the writer has rather strong emotions about the subject and thinks John behaved poorly. In the descriptive report, the official received facts: the who, what, when, where, and how.

It is also important for the judicatory official to know:

1. The history of the problem, that is, is it new or of long standing? Has this individual behaved in a similar fashion before?
2. Are any others involved, or just one individual?
3. How well known is the situation to the membership?
4. Can the leadership be counted on to be supportive in any confrontational actions?

Other information may be pertinent in a particular situation, or within the context of specific denominational procedures.

In those unfortunate instances when the pastor is the source of antagonism, bringing in available denominational help may be the only recourse lay leadership has. In churches with a presbyterian or episcopal polity, this means contacting an official of the presbytery or diocese, for example. In strictly congregational churches it might mean bringing the matter before the congregation itself— as the highest recognized authority for dealing with such problems. Even in the latter case, denominational officials can and often do have significant advisory and consultive functions. One caution when a *pastor* is apparently antagonistic: be sure of your facts before escalating the situation to the denominational level. For a pastor, the stakes are very high: his or her reputation, livelihood, and perhaps even vocation are at issue. Recognize, too, that such an action on your part is going to make you vulnerable to attack, perhaps resulting in your being unfairly subjected to discipline or even being forced out of the congregation.

Four final points are worth emphasizing, and these are directed to denominational officials themselves. First, do not be afraid to use the power that has been vested in you. One problem that congregations experiencing antagonistic conflict repeatedly report is the hesitancy of judicatory officials to use whatever authority is appropriate to their denomination, whether that means rendering a decision after hearing out the problem, or consultation only.

Second, economic and political considerations should in no way determine your response to or the just resolution of a situation. Congregations must be confident that judicatory officials will not allow themselves to be manipulated (by circumstances or by the antagonist) into expediency-based decision making.

Third, prepare in advance. Develop policies, procedures, and responsible personnel that enable you to be the resource your congregations need. Otherwise you will always be playing catch-up, reacting to situations rather than providing help in advance.

Fourth and finally, in addition to helping in the midst of crises, denominations should also encourage education for preventive purposes. A few denominations have already established training programs to instruct pastors and lay leaders in how to handle antagonism before an antagonistic conflict erupts in earnest. More denominations are likely to follow suit. As a minimal ideal, every judicatory body ought to recognize this responsibility for preventive education and training. This might involve regional workshops or use of this book and its study guide at the local congregation level. Each denomination ought to have one person with responsibilities for both the handling of antagonistic situations and the fostering of education for congregations.

Whether you are a pastor, lay leader, or denominational official, apply these principles as best you can within the guidelines of your particular denomination. May the Lord bless you with the innocence of doves and the wisdom of serpents as you pick your way through this territory.

To Leave or Not to Leave

WHEN you are embroiled in conflict with an antagonist, you may feel like Job:

O that my vexation were weighed, and
all my calamity laid in the balances!
For then it would be heavier than the
sand of the sea (Job 6:2-3).

Experiencing an attack from an antagonist can crush your spirit, diminish your sense of personhood and self-worth, and even threaten your attachment to the church. You may have a spectrum of feelings ranging from anger, frustration, confusion, and depression to fatigue, tension, and total discouragement. These feelings might lead you to wonder, "What am I doing here? Should I leave or stay?"

Whether you are a lay leader, simply a church member, or a staff person, that is not a question to be answered without first going to God in prayer to know his will.

Listed below are several reasons to stay, and a few that might suggest leaving. Test all of them against your perception of God's will for you, your family, and the congregation.

Hang in There

When negative emotions wreak havoc with your life and giving up seems like the best of bad alternatives, I have three words of advice: *Hang in there!*

I encourage you not to resign prematurely, or for church members, not to leave too quickly. I know too many pastors and church leaders who precipitously resigned because of an antagonist when it was neither necessary nor helpful. Resigning prematurely, or leaving, can hinder God's mission and ministry in your congregation.

I don't deny that some situations will call for resignation. "Hang in there" would be quite inappropriate advice for someone about to be lynched. This chapter discusses situations in which continued ministry would be impossible. However, in most cases there are very good reasons for seriously considering "hanging in there."

• *The solution is usually temporary.* When a church leader relinquishes his or her position, the solution is often temporary. Once a replacement arrives, the problem begins again. Although the antagonist may skip over the next leader to let things cool down, he or she will later resume the offensive. Remember that an antagonist's continuing aggressive behavior originates within him- or herself; you just happen to be the most convenient target at the time. A resignation can also allow the antagonist to feel reinforced and to become more firmly entrenched in a congregation.

• *100% support is rare.* Hanging in there is difficult when you think others are against you, but consider the following statistics. According to Gallup polls, one of the most popular presidents in American history was Franklin Roosevelt, who, at the peak of his popularity in January, 1942, had 84 percent of the citizens' support. This means that 16 percent were *not* in agreement with his policies and practices. Most presidents have received 40-60 percent support as a rule; for some, public support has sunk far lower at times. Even presidents with less than 30 percent support did not resign. Some church leaders, though, find it an unpalatable reality that not every living soul in the congregation will support them. No one *ever* has 100 percent support of 100 percent of the people 100 percent of the time. Don't let the lack of complete support shake your self-confidence. You might well have more support than you realize. In truth, the vocal minority remains a minority, despite their volume. As Ulysses S. Grant said, "There are always more of them until they are counted."

• *It probably isn't your fault.* The antagonist is generally the offending party, and this is another important reason to hang in there. If anyone should leave or resign, it should be the antagonist, not the church leader. When I consult with judicatory officials and congregations involved in antagonistic situations, I always ask this question: "Has this individual ever done anything like this before?" Often astonished realization dawns when I ask this question. They usually say something like: "Why, yes, come to think of it, this person does have a long history of that behavior." Normally I don't even need to point out the significance of that repetitive pattern.

• *It's not just your problem.* Another reason to remain is that the antagonist is not your problem alone. It is imperative for you and other leaders to recognize that the behavior of the antagonist is a *congregational* problem that affects the whole congregation.

• *Personal and family needs.* Consider personal and family needs. This may seem more important for paid church staff, but other church leaders should take note as well. Consider your family. Tearing up roots can be traumatic for children. Perhaps you have a teenage child near graduation, or maybe your spouse has a new job, an enjoyable one with excellent benefits and job satisfaction. Suppose you recently purchased a house. Ask yourself, "How will resignation affect my family?" More to the point,

"Can I let this antagonistic individual determine my life choices?"

• *Moral responsibility.* Deciding to vacate your position also involves questions of moral responsibility. Being a church leader involves certain responsibilities to the people you serve, to your family, and to yourself. More importantly, you are responsible to God to do what is right and truthful. Mordecai's words to Queen Esther are pertinent here: "And who knows whether you have not come to the kingdom for such a time as this?" (Esther 4:14). *You* may be the one destined to put an end to the antagonistic problem, and resigning may be a symptom of the Jonah syndrome—running away from God's will.

Your success as a leader depends largely on your ability to be self-directed and God-directed, rather than depending exclusively on feedback from others. If you only look to others for validation, you will assuredly run into problems. It is far better to be somewhat lonely than to allow your entire sense of self-worth to depend on others. Distance clears the head for sound decisions.

If Leaving Becomes Necessary

Although resignation is usually unnecessary, it is still one alternative. I hope it doesn't come to that for you. For lay leaders, the option is not as grave as for church staff. Lay leaders may need to vacate their position, or sometimes leave the congregation altogether. For pastors and other church professionals, however, resigning also threatens loss of income and frequently necessitates moving to a new location. Resignation can also mean changes for the church professional's family—children uprooted, spouses' careers disrupted, good friendships ended. The decision to resign is never reached lightly.

Since the decision to resign is often made in circumstances less than conducive to clear thinking, I would like to present what I consider to be *good* grounds for resigning in an antagonistic situation, and then discuss procedures for resignation.

• *Reasons for resigning.* The basic issue for you to consider is whether or not you have lost effectiveness as a leader in your church setting.

Consider resigning if you have made many serious mistakes or committed great (and actual) offense. If your behavior will result in scandal and offense, or, if the charges an antagonist has brought against you are true, then moving on might be the only self-respecting course of action.

Consider resigning when a significant majority is against you. Although you might be primarily in the right, continuing to function in your position becomes difficult at best when most of the members of your group or congregation have lined up against you. You could be in that rare situation where there are so many antagonists and followers that nothing you do could change the situation. Resignation is certainly appropriate in this instance.

Consider resigning when you have lost effectiveness as a leader. Even if you weathered the storm and came through with majority support, resignation may be the expedient and caring action. Your presence might simply be an unpleasant reminder of that time of strife. But do not give up too soon. You might be surprised by the recuperative powers of individuals. Time will tell if you suffered a permanent loss of effectiveness. If the unrest increases as time passes, then perhaps you should move on.

Consider resigning when staying poses a risk to your physical or emotional health. If the stress you experience from an antagonistic situation is a major factor (or you suspect it may be) in causing dangerous health problems, don't dally.

Consider resigning when one or more judicatory officials in all love and honesty recommends it. This last instance applies more to church professionals than to lay leaders. Judicatory officials deal with such matters frequently, and therefore speak from a wellspring of experience. Listen to their reasons; hear them out. In some denominations, you have no choice but to comply with their wishes; in others the decision is technically left in your hands. Either way, give their advice a great deal of prayerful thought.

• *How to resign.* When you have considered these factors well, and if resignation seems proper to you, here are some possible ways to proceed.

Be honest. Your honesty can educate your constituency. At first, they might wince at your candor. Speak out clearly, without cringing, however, because your frankness may well have an overall healthy effect. I know of one congregation that went through four pastors before one was assertive enough to confirm openly what most suspected: he (like the others) was leaving, not because God was calling him elsewhere, but because of an exceptionally obnoxious antagonist.

Leave no time bombs behind when you resign. Do all you can to smooth the transition to a new leader. While giving honest feedback, don't stoop to the level of name-calling or mud-slinging.

Arrange for an exit interview with appropriate leaders. They have a right to be fully informed as to your reasons for leaving. You owe it to them and to the group or congregation as a whole. You yourself can also learn from such an interview.

If you were the victim, resign your office according to a schedule that suits your convenience. Of course, if you were in the wrong yourself, you are well-advised to move on as soon as possible.

Apologize sincerely if, in any way, you are to blame for what has transpired. Confess boldly and ask for forgiveness from those you offended. This might be done before the congregation (especially if you are resigning as a pastor or a church staff person), or before the committee or board on which you serve. In short, apologize before the appropriate people.

Resignation almost always seems to be the lesser of evils, but most of the time it creates more problems than it solves. It is never an easy choice, and calls for a great deal of prayer, thought, and personal struggle.

The Aftermath

*I*T'S over, at least the worst of it. The long, arduous battle with a wolf in sheep's clothing has finally ended. As you and the other shepherds survey the landscape, reminders of the struggle meet your eyes. Tufts of wool dot the ground. The flock is scattered. Some sheep are gone for good; many still with you are limping and bleating for attention. Others mill about uncertainly. Still others have wandered away from the main flock with a determined look that says, "You'll have to do a lot of gentle coaxing to convince me to join you again." And some sheep are cropping grass contentedly, apparently oblivious to the struggle that has taken place.

As you gaze out over the flock you wonder how you and the other shepherds can nurture the sheep back to health again. You yourself took some nasty bites and bruises and need healing as well.

Care for Others

In the aftermath of an antagonistic situation, there are many who need care. Certainly the other leaders on the front line of attack have emotional sores that require prompt, caring treatment. What they probably need as much as your listening ear is encouragement. They need to hear, "You did well; we never could have done it without you." Such listening and affirmation go a long way toward helping them sort out their jumbled feelings.

Aside from the frontline casualties, there are also civilian injuries. Offer care to the confused, innocent bystanders, members who might be at a loss to understand what happened. Probe the depth and severity of each injury, opening the way for counsel and ministry to those who need it. Some wounds might turn out to be less serious than others, so it is important to match the varied needs with the proper amount of caring.

The followers who fell in with the antagonist also require care. Most likely, they are feeling qualms of realistic guilt. It is important not to gloss over that guilt with a superficial, "Oh, that's all right!" They know it is not "all right," and so do you. When you care for them, first give them ample opportunity to express their guilt. Once they have worked through their guilt and other emotions, then offer the soothing balm of forgiveness that assures full acceptance back into the fold. (You are not withholding forgiveness here, but simply avoiding the cheapening of it to the point of valuelessness.)

Finally, there are those victims of the controversy who seem to be overlooked so frequently—the ones who reacted to the stress by becoming inactive. They desperately need caring ministry, but the difficulty of caring for those who left is that their trust level is low. A visit from you or another leader will tangibly demonstrate concern. As they begin to understand that you care, they might open up and let you tend their wounds too.

The list of casualties needing care could be lengthened, but instead I urge you to look around. You'll see everyone who needs care, with one possible exception. Looking around, you might inadvertently miss an individual in direct need of care: yourself.

Care for Yourself

In numerous conversations with individuals who have suffered antagonistic attacks—both clergy and lay—I have discovered one constant: *not once did a church leader mention caring for self as part of the aftermath.* After an antagonistic ordeal, *you* need to experience healing as well. In Chapter 14 I discussed the value of a confessor-confidant during an antagonistic attack. After it is all over you might also find this counsel equally beneficial. There is also value in seeking counseling.

Whatever you decide to do, take yourself into account. You can't keep pouring care out of an empty cup, and you can't give to others what you haven't received yourself.

Let the Past Be the Past

Don't continually dredge up buried memories. Those who weathered an antagonistic battle together can be genuinely tempted to refer to it constantly or joke about it incessantly. Continually conjuring up the ghosts of antagonists can become downright wearisome. Repeated allusions to the antagonist, whether in jest or in anger, can strain relationships. Do all you can to limit that behavior.

Likewise, bringing up the matter before the congregation can be tantamount to rubbing salt into the wounds of the flock. For example, the idea of holding a healing service to purge the whole episode might seem appealing. Most of the time, though, this kind of review is equivalent to picking at a scab—which formed as the body's natural mechanism to promote healing.

Yet focusing on the present and the future does not mean failing to take protective measures. The recovery period is the ideal time to consider realistically how to avoid a repeat performance. For example, if the constitution or by-laws of the congregation are unclear or have a significant gap through which the antagonist walked with ease, now is the time to update them, making them less subject to manipulation.

Now is also a good time for leaders to learn more about the whole area of antagonism. The aftermath of an antagonistic attack will find congregational leaders especially willing to learn.

Your objective should never be merely to restore the congregation to its former state. On the contrary, from the first moments when you and the other leaders begin to gather the scattered flock, your goal should be to create an even healthier congregation. In my practice as a psychologist, I am not content merely to get my clients back on an even keel, to help them return to where they were before some crisis precipitated their coming to me. A psychologist friend of mine views himself not as a "head shrinker" but a "head expander." A congregation whose only goal is to recover and maintain its former stability is already slipping behind.

God's church is constantly on the move, bravely following the Master. The Good Shepherd knows sheep: fresh pastures are a requirement. Left too long to work over the same pasture, sheep crop the grass to the roots and kill it. God keeps his flock on the move to supply fresh, green pastures watered by deep streams. So, putting aside what lies behind and reaching toward what lies ahead, your congregation can be strengthened, growing into the fullness that God intends.

Relating to the Antagonist after It's All Over

Through concerted efforts, you and the other church leaders have met the challenge of the antagonist's attack. What stance do you now take toward the antagonist? How do you relate to that person now that it's all over? You might wish he or she would simplify your life by leaving the congregation, but it probably won't happen. What do you do then? Much of Chapter 13, "How to Relate to Dormant Antagonists," also applies after the situation is under control. The guidance that follows builds on the foundation laid there.

As a Christian, wiping the slate clean and starting over fresh will probably be uppermost in your mind after an antagonistic situation has ended. Were it only ordinary debate and disagreement now ended, even accompanied by a great deal of acrimony, I would unhesitatingly issue a hearty amen to that. But an antagonist unfortunately requires a different approach. You still need to forgive, but your forgiveness must not be blind. Offer your forgiveness with open eyes and a functioning memory.

A woman whom I know provides a helpful analogy. She thinks that every road is the Indianapolis 500. She has lost her license three times. Do I forgive her for her driving behavior? Certainly, even including the one (and *only*) hair-raising time I rode with her some years ago. But that does not mean I would want my children to ride to summer camp with her. And even though she may now have everything cleared up with the authorities, I would still not choose her to drive a bus full of children.

The same rationale makes sense with an antagonist. Be forgiving, but for your congregation's sake, don't be forgetting!

You need to be aware of the fact that there is no such thing as a "former" or "past" antagonist. A more accurate term might be *antagonist in remission*—an antagonist who, though active in the past, is at the present time inactive. An antagonist can be compared to a volcano. A volcano is a volcano whether it rumbles, spewing rock and ash, or appears silent and serene, puffing a little smoke now and then. Don't be duped by all that serenity. What is happening on the surface is not as important as what is churning about inside. In dealing with a dormant antagonist, be every bit as careful as you would in dealing with a volcano that erupted a year or two earlier.

In short, relapse is extremely common with antagonists, whether we like it or not.

Be cautious. Don't be surprised by relapses to antagonism and, of course, you and other leaders need to do all you can to prevent this from happening. You will want to combine your duty of being watchful with your responsibility to pray for the antagonist.

The Last Temptations

W HEN you turn the final page and finish this book, you will face the temptation to shelve what you have learned along with the book itself. It is always difficult to cross the bridge from speculation to action. Beneath that figurative bridge lives a whole family of trolls who will try to waylay you with reasons why you should not cross to the other side. The only way to silence these creatures is to confront every rationalization they offer with the truth. The truth, like the sun, will turn such trolls into harmless stones. Here are the lies those trolls will whisper and the truths you can bring to bear against them.

Troll #1: "You don't really think it will work, do you?"

As you read through this book, you probably heard from this troll more than once. A variation of this seductive blandishment is: "Maybe it would work for someone else, but not for you—it's not your style." This troll will insist, for example, that meeting with an antagonist whenever and wherever the antagonist wants will go farther to help the situation than meeting with an antagonist at the time and place you determine. This troll might also whisper that keeping an antagonist as busy and involved as possible on a board or committee is the best thing to do—that the antagonist will be so busy he or she will not have time to be antagonistic. These are seductive lies.

Troll #2: "You don't want discomfort, do you?"

Dealing effectively with antagonists entails involvement in situations where conflict necessarily takes place. The troll is right: nobody *wants* to experience uncomfortable conflict. Despite the fact that many times conflict is necessary and results in healing and greater justice, this troll is enough to scare many off. The best way to deal with it is to say: "I have made up my mind to do *right*, not what is comfortable, and the likes of you shall never dissuade me."

Troll #3: "People are never as bad as all that, are they?"

After you complete this book, this troll will still be around, insisting that you are too judgmental. The key to silencing this troll is to lay the facts out on the table: "Okay, Troll #3, we'll let the *facts* decide if Person X is an antagonist. Let's go back to Chapters 5, 7, 8, and 9 and see." Before you finish speaking, the troll will be silenced for good, and you can move on past it.

Troll #4: "People won't like you if you do these things."

Ouch! This troll knows how to hit where it hurts. No one likes to be disliked. You can silence this beast by pointing out that the popularity you may lose will only be short-term, and in all probability you will elicit the longer-term respect of many individuals. On the other hand, if you give in to the troll's temptation, your popularity will only be short-lived, followed by loss of respect and numerous other losses in the long run.

Troll #5: "Shepherds don't attack."

This troll is wrapping two lies in three words. First, it is misrepresenting what you are advised to do in this book. Your goal is not to attack the antagonist, but to defend the flock. By rendering the antagonist harmless or ejecting him or her from the flock, you accomplish this. The troll's second lie is a false conception of what a shepherd or leader is all about. The chief job description of a shepherd is that he or she cares for sheep. Certainly that caring may involve some unfortunate but necessary "assertiveness" toward wolves, whether they come at the flock from the outside—howling and growling, with fangs gleaming—or whether a wolf has dressed in sheep's clothing and infiltrated the flock.

Troll #6: "No one will support you in this."

This is a difficult one, and in some ways may be the biggest temptation you will face. You know what could be done, and you know what could be done if the corporate leadership of the congregation works together: antagonists would never acquire any momentum. You also know how much mission and ministry is impeded when other leaders are noncooperative. You may feel alone, without support. Some of these feelings may be realistic; some may be unrealistic. All this taken together may give this troll ammunition to tempt you to push aside authentic activity and join the crowd. The only problem is that this may cause greater pain than doing the right thing. So tell this troll that even if others don't go along with you, you must exercise your responsibilities. Selling out and going along with the crowd is not for you.

Troll #7: "But it's so much work!"

That's right. Dealing with antagonists involves much effort. It is hard work to change old habits and form new behaviors, especially when you are involved in a crisis situation. You as leader will need to exert much self-discipline, which for some individuals will not come naturally. But you can tell this troll (and yourself) that if you don't work hard now, there may be nothing left to work for later. So tell it to get lost.

This book began with hope, and so shall it end. The optimism and desire of so many Christians is that God will make everything all right in the end—and so he shall, but the end is not yet. While we wait in the certain hope of the Lord's return, we must keep on keeping on.

You are at the end of the bridge. Action is only a step away. I can't walk with you into the land ahead. I can only cheer you on. And may God be with you.